IN THE COMPANY OF WOMEN

An Anthology of Wit & Wisdom, Sass & Class

Edited by Apryl Skies & Alicia Winski

Edgar & Lenore's Publishing House
13547 Ventura Boulevard
Sherman Oaks CA 91423
eappublishing@gmail.com

In the Company of Women:
An Anthology of Wit & Wisdom, Sass & Class

Apryl Skies & Alicia Winski © 2011
All rights reserved.

No part of this book may be reproduced, stored in a
retrieval system or transmitted by any means without
the written permission of the publisher and/or author.

Printed in the United States of America

Editing and Cover Design by Apryl Skies
Co-Editing by Alicia Winski

ISBN-13: 978-0578102481
ISBN-10: 057810248X
Library of Congress Control Number: 2012934434

www.EdgarAllanPoet.com

Table of Contents

Introduction   8

A Conversation in Survival   9

In the Company of Women   10

Of Clouds & Clarity   12

Waiting for Red Wings to Stir   13

This Mother's Sentiment   14

In the Kitchen with Dovey   15

Breath Beneath the Surface   16

woven like the night   18

Eighteen   19

My Birth   20

Like Tamagotchis   21

My Poem Walked Through the Door   22

Deliverance   23

The Unexpected   24

Novitiate Psalms   26

She Set Sail   27

Wishblue   28

maiden mother crone   29

The Sum of Her Parts   30

The Liquid Metropolis I/VII   31

I Have Moved Away   32

To My Mother   33

Elevations: I   34

Psalms to a Daughter   36

Thirst   37

My Unsung Heroine   38

In the Company of Women: A Blood Bloom to Hold   40

Through Varied Veins   42

Vermillion   43

Yadira's Arms   44

Hands Full of Curious   45

In Her Hair   46

Tabitha   48

While Baubie Sleeps   50

My Love	51
To Mom with Love	52
Warmth on a Cold Day	54
We Called Her Nana	56
'tis You, my Friend	57
The Write Word	58
South-bound Soaring	60
Portrait of an Aunt	61
Halved	62
Pieces of You	63
Granny	64
She Knows a Recipe for Jam	68
Family Reunion	69
The Empty Women	70
Wild Ponies/Women in Chains	72
Division of Sound vs Matter	73
American Beauty	74
Porn Star	76
Porno Woman	78
Happy V Day	80
Thorna Eldritch: Shadow of a Self Portrait	86
That Hot Afternoon	87
Like God	88
Dark Muse	90
Night Fever	91
To Heather After Nine Years of Friendship	92
As Girlfriend Do	93
Second Chance	94
Ma Ze	97
Birthday Lunch Autopsy	98
Bella	102
She Sits on the Landing	103
The Master	104
The Pen & the Pearl	106
To You, Anaïs	108
A Kidnap	112
Edna St. Vincent Millay's Apartment	114

A Conversation with a Dying Romantic   117

A Scarcity of Lazarus, Who is She?   118

Do the Black Poppies Still Hear You Sing?   120

Musemagik*   121

Confessions: III   122

Woven Into Me   125

Clairvoyant   126

On the Conjuring of Devils   129

Vanda   132

Beneath Silence   133

brokenwing   134

Cat Eyes & the Tragedy of Mother   135

Regressions: IV   136

The Great Escape   138

Mommy   140

Hands   141

Dear Mother   142

Forgiveness on the Tongue   143

In Aftermath   144

In All Fairness   146

Coming Home   148

Getting to the Heart of the Matter   150

In the Company of Women   151

My Breast   152

Mimic   153

Saying Goodbye   156

'night Mother   157

For Alicia   158

The Mathematics of Division   159

In the Company of Women   160

Acknowledgments   162

Introduction:

"I am a story…" Cklara Moradian

IN THE COMPANY OF WOMEN broke the mold right out the poetic gate…a collection of carefully selected poetry, short story and memoir with so many facets, this body of work seems almost difficult to define.

From suburban backgrounds to groundbreaking histories of the oppressed; this colorful anthology reveals personal truths by women of yesterday, today and tomorrow. The literature contained within contradicts the conception of feminine frailty with simple beauty, complex emotion and the catharsis of survival and sustenance.

Every woman is a story and whether dynamic, humorous or tragic, this collection is an intimate look at relationships between women, female bonds and the effect of these interactions upon their lives and complicated sensibilities.

This is not exclusively a tribute to a mother's love, sister bonds or close friendships between women, but rather a testament of strength, experience and humor hidden in the awkward moments of realization, the epiphany of cyclic change or the confrontation toward what many women feel helpless to change. There is hope and tragedy in truth, beauty and wisdom in experience and this balance is the essence of what defines our histories.

Within this archive, poet Gloria Wimberley and author Apryl Skies approach their experience with whimsy, hope and compassion, while writer Alicia Winski reigns as *Queen of Brutal Honesty*, delivering an abrupt literary snakebite. Wanda Morrow Clevenger is a refreshing dose of sagacity and poetic undertone, brimming with nostalgia and creativity. Barbara Moore is always a bullet into fruit, taking a poignant approach to the poetic path, never a dull blade. Cklara Moradian; a human rights activist has broken through the confines of human cruelty, urging us all to live by peaceful means and grander intention. Each of these voices, along with the many others included, welcome you to experience the many journeys shared within.

With much love and inspiration we thank you for holding this collection of life moments in your hand and invite you to celebrate our experiences IN THE COMPANY OF WOMEN.

A Conversation in Survival

Sometimes
to survive
you need fists

sometimes
to survive
you need to play dead

sometimes
to survive
you need to come together…

Alicia Winski & Apryl Skies

In the Company of Women

Had I been asked to write about my friendships with women many years ago, I assure you my perspective would be *oceans* opposite.

The relationships I had with females growing up were certainly no testament to the strong ties of sisterhood. Despite sincere efforts and best intentions, trusting other dames proved challenging. Surrounded by those who bullied me, I became introverted growing a tough outer shell, one very hard to crack. Worse still, was being made to feel inferior by the very females who declared themselves friends.

Growing tired of the shallow nature of the young women I encountered and the realization that most were out to squeeze my emotion dry, I began to relate more to the platonic relationships with males. The sincerity I found in these relationships helped to heal my heart and I was finally able to gain a healthier self esteem.

It wasn't until my adult life did I become more open to relationships with other women. Each of these relationships are of a unique light and I couldn't imagine life without them. Number one being Alicia Winski, my poetry sister whom without, this anthology would have never come about.

Besides writing, hiking is one of my most precious past times and I thank Helena, Monique & Kim for being such an inspiration to me. It is the times when we push ourselves beyond the limit, breathe in and look out at the beautiful landscapes of California when I feel so truly blessed. We have scaled mountains together, taken it to the extremes and this is impossible to do without mutual trust.

As I get older and hopefully more wise, I have grown to appreciate the relationships with women in my life far more than I could have ever expected. I discovered a sacred credence and support in my female friends and the ability to actually trust again has lead me down a path of personal growth...Lessons learned, hope shared and forgiveness gained in the company of women.

With all seriousness aside...dirty martini anyone? Cheers!

In the company of women
I have found lasting friends...

as I grow older
become a bit bolder,
molded by time and ideals,
I gain perspective
by the things life reveals
between the pages and the dust
beyond the darkness and mistrust...

Through vacant skies
or tragic good-byes,
making memories, sharing histories
whether sun, wind or thunder,
beneath the sky we're under...

I am blessed to have found friends
in the company of women.

Apryl Skies

11

Of Clouds & Clarity

A veil of smoky blue velvet
lifts in my mind
to waft out wispy
motes of memories:
My grandmother's smoke-rings
formed an ethereal nimbus
above her sister's head...

In the nearby dimly-lit living room,
I watched the life-is-perfect Brady Bunch
on TV in the 70's,
they laughed & chatted,
sipped beer in the afternoon,
smoked Salems,
played Yahtzee for hours,
sat in uncomfortable metal chairs
in a cramped kitchen
--never complained
about simple, yet satisfying lives
in the kelly-green hills of Appalachia
(a small Brickyard Bend town in West Virginia)

Even when my oft-lucid great-aunt
joked and smiled through
an especially trying MS haze
~~a plume of plaintiveness
rising in Bobby Vinton's voice
on the radio as he crooned,

She wore bluuuuuueeee velvet...

Their sun-burnished glint
of silver lining never turned dark
never turned ashen grey

Gloria J. Wimberley

Waiting for Red Wings to Stir

The long light of September slants
through the small window of a back door.....
its amber glow creeps
across the stale air of a darkened kitchen
.........to touch........a simple blue teapot......waiting.....for company.......
visitors you would treat more graciously
than members of your own family.

In this haze of mixed messages I grew naked,
too cold to penetrate the bitter ice,
that blue zone carved featureless
which hung........porcelain fragile......between us.

You, my mother, inherited a time
of torn pages, a language,
which did not permit that wild passion of red
to blossom into its own unique shape.
Instead you grew old sitting with that simple blue teapot
........waiting........,
feet arthritic and swollen
against linoleum worn thin
by the feet of your grandchildren.

I never did know if you understood
that sharp blue edge which held you hostage.....
........just beyond recognition.......

Peggy Anne Larson

13

This Mother's Sentiment

What will you say of me?
When only words will possess
what is left on this plane of dust
and wind-blown collections?

This truly is of little importance,
my Dearest Child.

Just love me today,
remember my God, my hands, my heart,
these arms
and always the hope
we held together.
For at times,
it was the best we had.

Sadie Harris

In the Kitchen with Dovey

The kitchen was the safest place
to be with my mother.
It was all about food:
the making, the serving, the eating.

As a child I would boost myself up
onto the gray tile counter in the corner nook
between the pink stove and the porcelain sink.
Behind me, cupboards full of cereal boxes,

rigatoni noodles, Uncle Ben's rice, dried onion soup mix,
and matzo meal. To my right, another cupboard
from where I would dispense upon request onion or
garlic powder, cinnamon, paprika, and Lawry's seasoning salt.

I learned all her recipes: her brisket, her noodle kugel,
her schnitzel, her salmon patties, and of course,
her chicken soup. Standing next to her at the stove,
I watched her lean over the tall pot of soup, tasting

the piping hot broth for flavor. Then skimming
the top of the soup, saving the chicken fat
to make schmaltz, best schmeared over a slice of challah.
Nothing was ever measured, always mixed by look,
feel, and taste. Feeding a family of eight was a grand feat.
For me, it was an education nestled beside the hips of the master.

Melissa Grossman

Breath Beneath the Surface

Rosella Beard with Twila
December 19, 1912 – December 26, 1990

A rounded woman with plain features and squared jaw and tightly waved hair who cooked from scratch and from memory – leftover fried chicken, drained on newsprint, sat out in humid summer hours until the evening meal, tempting those remaining guests who never once fell ill of botulism – whose features mirror acutely in her passel of offspring, is the woman I should have wanted to know better.

The sober woman born the year of *Titanic* – who neglected to mention such an enthralling tidbit – had no middle name. Very many tidbits breathed life beneath the surface waiting a late impart.

A cordial woman who subscribed to yearly perms for her youngest daughter already endowed with natural curls, the whisperer of gossip three feet above the grandchildren because *little pitchers have big ears*, banished a dallier and home nursed a second husband until fate called.

The authoritative woman who shrilled when this little girl rummaged through her purse and broke a red lipstick, squealed "Yahtzee" with the same verve, laughed from her soul around every holiday table, was not stopped by a head-on car collision.

A firecracker who let slip mischief when she sang "Roll me over in the clover, lay me down and do it again" could next flare for reasons only she discerned – tempest in a Fire-King teacup.

The strong woman who succumbed to a cracked furnace at the age of seventy-eight – found frozen solid in the garage – might have thought to keep and take so many secret things with her.

An eighteen-year-old birthing my mother, alone in her upstairs bedroom, who wrapped the baby in sheets to present to unmindful parents on Christmas morning; the curious woman saying "Look what Santa brought" is the same, had I an inkling, I should have pressed to know better.

Wanda Morrow Clevenger

woven like the night

a woman told me her story...

she sat on her thr(one)
of secret and uncertainty
as the babe in the basket
drifted away on the tide~
woven like the night

she could have died...

labored breaths, a soft
cry into darkness - hers
a leaf rustles in its place
born like tender light

he n(ever) belonged to her...

Apryl Skies

Eighteen

Eighteen, Strong willed,
ill equipped
relentless
Daisy is her name
popping out a baby girl
December 10 many moons ago

Unwilling to give up her child
unwed, single teenage Mom
emerged in the 70's
at a time when her friend's
were attending hooky parties
socializing and drinking
in tow with her child

Emigrating with her Mom and
siblings leaving behind her own
father in a land that offered them
no growth or hope
starry eyed, independent,
strong and fierce
gave way to resilience
during the most trying times

So when she was told she wasn't fit
to be a Mom, she was irresponsible,
she was reckless
in true defiance
she kept her baby
even long after the teenage dad
disappeared into the background

Annie Hilerio

My Birth

My eyes are closed I cannot move
something is around my neck
I feel restrained (it is tight in here)
I am scared something is wrong

I hear your voice, I feel your pain
we bond through a river of blood
I gasp for air, but yet, there is none
whispers outside say I am to blame

Please, I need you now
                        this is the time
this hurts, so come to me
I say it once
            I say it twice
Please, I want to be free

So much at stake, what is the price?
Just the thought of you holding me
I share my strength, so be brave
the day has come, can you see?

The truth has come,
I'm here to save
it's just you and me, you feel the flow
you push you scream you see me now
                you release a pain-free sigh . . .
you see me now, but I am blue
how could this be?

A prick, a poke, a slap on the ass

I scream.   I cry.   I am born~

Helena Hunter

Like Tamagotchis

This woman I admire the most
has rosettes for eyes, pink as asses
bathed too long, rubbed with talc.

This woman dangles orphans
in her plait, skirt hem and flip-flop beads,
smock pockets peg full, cash empty.

This woman drives a Volkswagen
that never breaks down, angels,
she says. And wind, I think.

This woman's eggs were stuck:
fifteen flushes, fifteen squirts
of bleach, fifteen fresh starts.

This woman speaks from her heart:
her words warm with a pulse.
She leaves them everywhere;

people like me left to nurture
them in our own lives,
like Tamagotchis, like babies.

Jacqui Corcoran

My Poem Walked Through the Door

My poem walked through the door
I couldn't ignore her
she was Mexican, an older woman
short and 9 months pregnant.
She asked if she could clean the windows
anything. Begged to clean the bathroom
anything.
She had an odor of desperation
she wanted to be worth something
anything.
Her pain dripped from her eyes.
My poem walked through the door
and needed a helping hand
she needed money
she said her husband was sick
she had more children at home
and her baby was due in one week.
My poem walked through the door
9 months pregnant, hungry and desperate.
I reached into the cash register
I took a five my boss would have killed me for taking
she would have screamed at me
we would've had a row...
I wanted to give her the whole till
I took the five, walked over to her
handed it to her as her tears fell
on my boss's beloved wooden floor
soaking into the grooves of the hard wood
I hugged her bent shoulders and big hard belly
So tight I'm surprised I didn't feel the baby
kick me, hard.
My poem was grateful and hugged me back
my poem was a desperate woman
my poem walked out the door

L. K. Thayer

Deliverance

"Take my hand, I promise, I won't let go"

Her diminutive voice quietly piercing through a heavy
veil of darkness; a tiny pinpoint laser leading a snapping,
snarling savage damned to cancerous confinement,
warily out into a light long dim

so frightened, so frightened

"Won't you please just trust me?" asked this little pilgrim,
 small persistence, stirring stagnant sensibilities—

Trust: a luxury stripped from life so very long ago,
a commodity no longer affordable to

a leery woman shell shocked by life, bled by betrayal,
scarred in treachery-
a rabid bitch biting hesitant hands of affection
lips stained with the blood of those who would love her

so lost, so lost

"Take my hand", she said to me,
"I promise, I won't let go" and this stray,

so wary, so weary

this maddened mute long silenced by despair,
a stilled voice unleashed into the arms of salvation,
found deliverance and revelation in the mischievous warm
eyes of this young stranger, Apryl Skies
and friendship forged in blind faith and trust …

was born …

Alicia Winski

The Unexpected

Under a firelight, shining distance
angels observe with wings spread wide
Orion arches his bow
above the hills of Los Angeles
and beneath this hazy sky,
where an unexpected stranger
enters Neptune's orbit,
love spills over like wine or April rain.

    In the air, a scent of something
    unexpected, destined, new.
    Somewhere an infant cries
    in this crowded, crumbling house,
    where its weary eves bend
    beneath this heavy dale of time
    and with the independence of St. Lucia
    a ghost wanders these narrow hallways,
    creaking the wooden floor boards and tells a tale,
    unfolding like a wailing accordion
    in this settled unquiet.

An old woman rocks in her chair
with, gray locks twisted tightly
like a cinnamon pastry,
her tiny frame swallowed up
By colorful quilts sewn
with two crooked, calloused hands.

    In the backyard orange groves bend
    bearing fruit, as the grapevine
    trolls the terrace in search of sun
    and beneath this February storm
    rabbits seek the dry-warmth refuge
    of handmade hutches, crafted of wire and wood.

This day arrives with joy and fear,
tears of uncertainty and celebration.
A bouquet of flowers
stands tall in the dining room
and in its smiling, bold beauty

    renders the poet a name.

Apryl Skies

Novitiate Psalms

Dry flowers chafe in a January vase
while I long for bouquets of early summer
wantonly riotous
from the Mennonite Market stall
where prim, unadorned girls
with soft assuaging hands
sort a beauty they must interiorize,
only their bare fingers know
the seductive sweetness.
Here in the white and grey nunnery of winter
a memory of awakening scandalizes
with the covert yearning for perfume and promise
softening the beds of earth
stretching long days of kindling light
seeming as a scene from an old cathedral painting
in an impressionist gallery
where barefoot suppliants tease toes
and drink the alcohol of flowers.

Katherine L. Gordon

She Set the Sail

She set the sail
to Southern shore
to catch a falling star *
she made the bend
on broken wing
and lifted voice to God.

Fear did rise
and doubt did reign
on many a stormy day
but now she sails on quiet sea
with stars above ablaze,
for courage came
on crested wave
      for girl with mended wing.

Pam Lampe

Wishblue

She says Life is...

sleeping like a stone
stained-glass keeper
etched in the brain
coral that eschews
the ghostly blue
sting of the man o' war
with his tenter-hook
tentacles silent
in search of flesh
to touch

"Meddy's" eyes ever cast down
to the mysterious depths of indigo
Mere Mer
so inked in myth and tidal pith

Like a mermaid-as-anchor
she sinks
to the water-weighted sand
closing her ethereal blue eyes
to the world...

Ms. Medusa sleeps heavily
--dreaming of touch
without the sting

Gloria J. Wimberley

maiden – mother – crone

the maiden

dreaming of a prince
to rescue me from childhood
wishes do come true

the mother

body your shelter
heart pumping love into you
be careful my child

the crone

your children I'll teach
these parts of me that live on
facets of my heart

Annie Brodrick

The Sum of Her Parts

My mother is a sculptor, making
dragons from clay. They lie
by the fireplace scaled and glazed,
lazy with heat, they never move.

My mother is a teacher;
introducing me to Shakespeare
Old Possum's Book of Practical Cats
Yeats and Yates and Ogden Nash.

My mother is a writer of
poetry vibrant, dark, intense.
Of myths and folklore
and fairytales.

Mornings I wake to find her
placing scones out on a tray
warming the kitchen for when we
come, bare foot and drowsy, into her light.

She is the richest language.
She is the deepest lake.

Sophia Argyris

The Liquid Metropolis 1/VII

The City, Art of its Beginning and its End

Her skin is a flash red salute,

Arrière!
        Assemblé
Avant!! Light in her chestnut horse hair, soon she will
settle into the green glass on the table, muted by cardinal
cloth of birth into the needled eye flash exposure.
Slow wine in her
blackened mouth. Caught in a
kiss of the past movement. A moment
dreaming of what the body's always wanted. A fragile silence
in the soft contours of a face, its touch.

Her language is a newborn's fist and sits in her chest
like a white tulip with stains of twilight hung and stretched
like a paper in cracks of cold windows, passing
and reflecting their kingdom of dusty memorabilia, bones
of small ghostly animals spitting ash into thin water sculptures of rain.

It will remain questionless.
Houses huddled together like small sisters in begging linen
gleaming into the vast paint of memory in the skies. The only
companions. Quiet witnesses of the shut door, unknockable.

Tomorrow
their stories will be repeated
and lost in a mouth of a dead man bleeding on cherry wood
with blossoms hidden and swelling inside, living for no one.

Petra Whiteley

I Have Moved Away

I have moved away half blind, my good eye kneeling,
forgetting the blue storm of its awkward gene(sis).
Passing from womb to wound
                                        a buried fist and a lie
that had no honeymoon but a fleeting grasp at tit,
and a fistful of dissolving summers picking at soft pavements.

        Launching helplessly from a child's dirt
all my hopes and absences proud as fire looking for a cloud
in time noticing the crows clever and the cats content,
the flowers blooming with the eyes of old women and the skirts of
maidens.

Each winter killed me a little because I could not love the ice
and had only printed skin for amour. Only skin,
like every papery human trying to remain intact
or acclimatize graciously to the summary of their scars. They say

scars are beautiful,
beautiful as moments in white dresses and combed hair
like all good brides with their glued pieces and their shadows.
Their bouquets yellow with spring: a dappled fugue –
a clump of memory and of loss.

Gillian Prew

To My Mother

There was never a day
that you stood with me
looking out of a door
dizzy
after bending down
to saw wood
and everything was golden
a golden haze
over
the green trees
and leaves turning
yellow and red
and the distant mountains looking
black.

Lois Michal Unger

Elevations: I

We are both learning
to take small unsteady baby steps,
I have spent an eternity
cripple backed and hunched from the world
now I do so willingly,
supporting two small hands-
she is to me as I
to her   guide ropes,
lashed together through a storm
of growing up and growing older,
(and I) of nearing the edge of a precipice
peering over the edge,
contemplating
what if...

...and then stepping back.

These are the bones of my
confession
            regression
                        elevation.

For now I cannot raise my eyes
from the ground,
they are pulled down by shame
shades of grey have washed over my sight
to prevent me from feeling,
appreciating the beauty as she pulls
at my invisible apron string.
I want to slap myself hard across the face,
stuff the dishcloth into my mouth
to stop me screaming.
But today I shall swallow down the bile
and melancholy fear
and breakfast

She is my bravery-
my love for her a medal pinned
to a ribbed chest where a heart
still beats   only just,
there is no justification
for it to cease in its appeal,
each beat pulses
                    live- live- live.

And we shall
through mist circling around the summit,
our lungs will fill with great spirals of
clean - fresh air,
sunrise shall burn a new day
clearing skies of mocking and self denial,
I will turn to offer a hand
to steady- support- to be declined.

Were I to face us both,
stood there in contemplation
I would see a reflection of two women-
full and
grown and
alive.

Samantha Ledger

Psalm to a Daughter

it's a pronouncement coldly, clinically delivered

> *a young girl lies in the bed she's made of pink*
> *patterned sheets stained with inebriating infatuation*
> *her future harbored in warm amniotic waters*

teenage idealism wavering, flourishing in hesitant anticipation,
she is an ambivalent pendulum swinging to and fro between fear
of the unknown and gratitude for the unexpected

> *heart strings and butterfly wings, a-flutter with contradiction*

summer dies, as does youthful complacency
winter delivers a child of a child into the arms of a woman

> *with birth comes damnation, with birth comes salvation*

exhausted body pillaged, womb ruthlessly plundered, an
aftermath of savage determination spews in ruby hues from
between quaking limbs while tender breasts are clutched
and clawed over a heart consecrated to infantile bondage

you will suffer pain and uncertainty
feel the prongs of betrayal and self doubt
you will be tempered in the fires of passion and
scarred by heartbreak and loss, but you

> *will never know what it means to walk alone*

tormentors will continue to torment the tormented
inhumanities will continue to be practiced by the inhumane
sisters will peel the flesh from bones over the most unworthy of men,
while brothers will bring anguish and despair down upon you, and

we will fail each other time and time again
let each other down in ways never to be understood
we will shed tear after tear after tear, but together we will overcome,

> *we will overcome, my daughter, and I will always love you...*
>   *Alicia Winski*

Thirst

Swollen knees buckle
drinking well distant, deadly
but her children thirst.

My Unsung Heroine

I am a story.

The year 1987,
in a detention center of an unnamed province.
A solitary cell, impregnated
with the body of a pregnant eighteen year old beauty.

The first noise I heard were her shouts,
as they threw her against the cemented walls of her cell.
The second sounds were the whispered humming
of her sweet soft lullaby, lulling me to sleep.

The third tones were of strange men and women,
speaking in tongues, demanding, shouting for hours,
but she would not give away.

The first thing I felt was fear,
as she was beaten on a long, thin wooden board,
the soles of her feet blistered from their lack of soul.

The second sensation was worry,
so I clenched my newly formed fists
hoping she could sense that she is not alone.

Then, our tears came streaming down
only mine swam within her protection,
the ocean of her womb.

The first taste on my palate was starvation.
She was not fed for days,
there was only the vacuum
of her apologetic umbilical cord.

The first nightmare I was forced to see
was her sleep deprived nights,
They bombarded her ear drums
with the beating sounds of women and young girls
pleading "No more!"

The first light I saw
was the bright, blinding darkness
of being born into shackles.

The first breath I inhaled,
was the scent of her strength.
The guards gave her weeks in a tiny cell with no toilet,
and she gave back a breathing, fighting, living being
all by herself.

She is- my mother
a prisoner of conscious.

I was a fetus, nourished and formed
by her tenacity and resilience,
and swam out of her womb into love.

Together we remain conscious,
and refuse to be tied down
to the cell blocks of memory.
Together we work for emancipation.

Cklara Moradian

In the Company of Women: A Blood Bloom to Hold

Nestled in my muse
of *matryoshka*
are minds
of minutiae
souls
in motes of light
voices
singing from the mouths
of unblinking doll faces
who wear babushkas
of varying shades
the verity of vermillion
~all looking (and feeling)
as true...as wondrous...as resilient
as heart-harkening
as red
as Stein's rose
standing in the warmth of rank and file

These women
petal-pained...
...yet stem-strong and leaf-lively
together
lift their smiling faces
skyward
to share-as-one
the corolla
of the sun

Gloria J. Wimberley

Through Varied Veins

From timid start, nerves taut with terror,
we have marched our trails of tears
and fears that mark precarious path.
We wobble-waver as we flounder-find
elusive balance in society, aboriginal
role of mother-matriarch discarded
on Christianity's callous horror-heap.
We wrap each other in empathy's embrace,
arms of red and white, black and yellow
intertwined in understanding of the grit
and grind and grace each day demands.
For this historic hike and haul requires
love and laugh and leaning, sisterhood's
support essential on such tiresome trek.
And whether we cover our hallowed heads
with burqa, babushka, or bandana, or let
straight or frizzy hair fly loosely bare
in breeze, we honour bond of birth and bone.
For blessèd blood of universal Oneness
circulates in sacred course through varied veins.

Carol Knepper

Vermillion

I
Saw
Her today
And was drawn
In by the unspoken
Story of Spanish eyes~
I wanted desperately to
Disregard all formality
And call her by
~Name~
To feel its vibrational music fall from my lips~She is
Vermillion against an indigo night~ A Cajun queen
Burning beneath the layers of beige~ A fiery
Curiosity that knows not her own
Effect~ I want
To see
Her
Spanish dancing with Punta hips~ A ruffling orchid
Of cayenne reds~ I glow like a Bombay sapphire
In witness of her unparalleled heat…
Because before all else
She came to
Be

~First she was a woman~

Leila A. Fortier

Yadira's Arms

I want those arms
yoga hand-stand
capoeira trained
rounded shoulder
bicep tricep like tree roots
crossed over one another
dancer's arms
baby toddler child- holding arms
sleeveless shirts
work in the garden arms
strong woman arms
cartwheel through life arms
I want those arms

R. V. Reyes

Hands Full of Curious

She came to me
quite pondering
in her youthful glow

Her hands full so of curious
a gathering of little dead things
locked in time-capsule gray
while embedded green stars
sparkled *"Why?..."*

Nothing lasts forever...

...how can you be sure?

She dug with bare fingers
a shallow hole in the earth
softly she placed them,
covering stiff creatures
with moist-cool soil

"Be still..." she said
as she dropped three daisies
upon them
and with a kiss
      she skipped away~

In Her Hair

Deep into the black
of each swallowed night,

my sister, 3 years old,
would perch on my knee like a

little peacock,
and I would rake my hands

through her long curly hair (beautiful
and splayed out like wings.)

I would comb that midnight-tangled mass
as she squealed

and slapped at my hands
with her little pink fingers.

I tugged at her hair in the summer,
the spring, and the fall,

but I tugged at her hair the hardest in the winter,
when the snow was angry.

The snow was always angry.

We would sit and listen in the dark,
(my hands in her hair,)

as the snow batted down our house
with its wide open fists,

as it violently vomited on our windows,
and then passed out
like a drunk in our yard.

We never understood how anyone could like that snow.

My sister now lives across the country
where the snow is gentle and rare.

Her hair is short now.
She does not remember that darkness,

or the way her hair looked
with my hands inside of it.

April Michelle Bratten

Tabitha

I met a little girl named Tabitha. There is a ball I must attend and it is far, far away. I will fly through the clouds, over the sun and over the ocean to a land as beautiful as this little girl who I'm about to see. I am going to Australia.

I was told she had long, blond hair, big blue eyes and a big beautiful smile. She is 5 years old with lots of love to give and she cannot see. Yes, you read right. She cannot see. Don't ask me why, don't ask me how, but she has already touched my heart and warmed my soul and the day has come when I will meet this angel. Before I go, I must find a special gift just for her. I don't know what it is, but when I see it I will know. From store to store, from block to block, I still don't find what I am looking for. With little time to go and one store left, I pray that it's here; this gift needs to be perfect.

"Oh goodness, oh gosh, oh what have I found?" A beautiful rain-stick with melted silver all over it! It was perfect! She can feel it, she can hear it, she will love it! The joy I feel within my heart to give it to this little girl is more than words can express. I asked the man at the register for the price and hear the saddening words "not for sale". My heart broke and my soul was crushed; I didn't know what to do. Seeing my transparent heart, he asked why I wanted to buy it and I told him the beautiful story of Tabitha and that it would have made the perfect gift for a beautiful, little blind girl. I expressed to him how much this meant. Then the man with jaw wide open replies, "Hold on please." He makes a phone call and then tells me a story "...the man that made this stick builds playgrounds for the blind." He insisted the rain-stick was on the house! With surprise and joy, I thanked him. With little time and still so far to go, I fly to meet this little, blue-eyed angel.

I am ready. I am here and I have the perfect gift. As I walk up the stairs and into the ballroom, I finally see Tabitha dressed in a purple gown, sliver shoes and a heart filled with warmth. We meet and she walks up to me, as pretty as can be. I tell her my name and tell her I have brought a gift, as special (as perfect) as she is. As I hand it to her, my heart beats hard; the moment I've been waiting for.

Her fingers slide down the stick, feeling the smooth silver, we tip it one way and the raindrops fall, she smiles. We tip it over again and listen while her fingers follow. Then she brings it up to her face and does it again. Her face lights up like sun and her aura brightens like diamonds. She took my hand and thanked me, finishing with a hug. She asked me if I would like to dance and it was like no one else was there. We turned and twirled and danced the night away...

There is a girl out there named Tabitha, special for just being her. She has touched so many hearts and this is just one story of how she touched mine, my story of Tabitha.

Helena Hunter

While Baubie Sleeps

for Sarah Fruchtnis Pauker (1880-1980)

Yesterday I found drawings I made of my grandmother
my *baubie* - as she slept, six months before she died.
It was the first time I had ever seen her still.
I used to plead with her to sit and visit.
She was always fussing, handing out *chatchkes*
from her gift stash, serving hot tea.
Not wanting to wake her, I took pencil to paper.
As I drew I listened to her breathing,
thought of her crossing the Atlantic
with her baby, my Aunt Clara in her arms.
Later widowed, with three young children,
she worked as a peddler
selling house-dresses door-to-door;
my mother helping her carry her wares.
I remember the torn toilet paper squares
she prepared every week before Friday *Shabbos*,
because strict Jewish law forbids
any kind of work on the Sabbath.
She once stayed up past midnight emptying
one-serving sugar packets into a jar.
Often I sat with her while she ate dinner in her room –
the same dinner every night: boiled chicken,
baked potato, steamed carrots. Sitting on the side
of her bed, the tray in front of her,
she would carefully skin and bone the chicken leg,
cut it into bite-size pieces, then peel the skin
off the potato, and mash it into the carrots.
When she awoke, I showed her my drawing
and I remember how the corners of her mouth lifted
like a gentle slice of pink melon.

Melissa Grossman

My Love
~For Rebekah, Caitlin & Katie

If ever you are all alone
and think that no one cares
pick up the quilt and count the stitch
for each was made with love

When you think the count complete
and that the job is done
remember there are many more
the ones that you don't see.

Love,

Grandma

Sheila Crawford

To Mom with Love

Your form left
maybe, spirit lingers
in heart's dwelling,
firmly ensconced

I see you in dress up time
In owned special
déjà vu moments
of us, you, me

Dad's brother said
I looked like him
others, like you
I am of you, my
own guardian angel

Always steering my
life's paper boat
out of harm's way
away from the brink

Flavor of soap
in my mouth still gags,
rinsing out
four letter words
innocently spoken

Wet rebuking eyes
still haunt when I am
less than thoughtful
and find myself

wanting in myriad ways
and then take
small steps in your ways
you were special to me
I was very special to you

My guilt pangs you
dismissed summarily as
growing pains, exhorted
never ever feel guilty
you were special,
you made me feel special

I remember you in waking
and in sleeping moments,
in all my roles
as daughter, mother, aunt
grandmother, friend.

Bina Gupta

Warmth on a Cold Day

Michael and I run home from school in the pouring rain. We don't look at each other, don't say the words, but we're hoping for the same thing - hoping Nanny will be there. Cold wet days are days for Nanny, mum's mum, the best grandmother in the world.

We can feel our school uniforms sticking to us, smell the stale wet wool of our blazers, feel our socks squelch in our hard shoes. Oh, please make Nanny be there.

We open the door together, not looking at each other, not breaking the silent spell.

"Come away in the pair of you. My, but you're soaked through." The tiny rounded frame appears before us, wrapping us in her arms. "God but I've missed you, it must be, what, three days ... have you grown? Let me see." The grin reveals the obligatory false teeth of her class and generation.

She bundles us into the living room, stripping us as we walk, discarding wet clothes as they fall from our tiny bodies. We stand in our underwear, grinning. The blankets are on the clotheshorse in front of the fire. She wraps us in the blankets, rubbing and hugging us in turn. She gathers up the wet clothes and puts them on the clotheshorse to dry, but she sets it off to the side leaving the blazing fire to colour our faces. We watch the orange flames and look around expectantly.

"What? What are you looking for? Did I forget something?" She's teasing us. We play along, shake our heads, pretend that there's nothing else we could possibly want. "Is it this?" She produces a tray from behind the couch. Two cups of hot orange and two slices of homemade gingerbread, dripping with butter.

We look at each other and grin, ease our arms out of the blankets and reach for the warming treats.

"My, but you're a sight for sore eyes, the pair of you." She grins at us, ruffles hair, rubs arms, kisses cheeks. We know she would eat us all up if she could - she's threatened it often enough.

We watch the steam rise from the wet clothes, savour the smells of the gingerbread and orange, enjoy the dark winter day, safe, warm, snug.

But there are more treats to come – she can't spoil us enough. Nanny runs a transport café in the Gorbals; it's a rough area, a hard life, but for us it has its compensations. Other Grannies bring a packet of sweets - ours brings the whole box. There are four of us, mind – the other two are at high school; they don't get home until later.

We know there are sweets somewhere, we just have to find them. If Papa has hidden them we're in trouble – he's too clever for us. Nanny makes it easy – she can't stand to see us struggle, she's had too much of that in her own life.

When we're warm enough to be free of our cocoons she lets us search. We snuffle like truffle pigs for our prize. Michael finds it in the cupboard under the stairs, beneath a pile of ironing. An entire box of Flying Saucers.

We give her huge hugs and she nearly squeezes the life out of us in return. She gives us one each. We put the little saucers in our mouths, feel the rice paper melt on our tongues and wait for the sherbet to tingle on our tongues. We laugh when the fizz starts and she tickles us to keep the laughter going. We have to beg her to stop.

We sit either side of her, cooried in, her warm hugs making the cold day seem so far away, and wonder what could be better than this.

Karen Jones

We Called Her Nana

We called her Nana, to distinguish her from our other grandmother.
Nana, my mother's mother was also called Emma.

Emma started the ball rolling
as far as a strong matri-lineal
line was concerned

not running in circles
her vibrant life
held meaning

in between the lines
of tradition (daughter of a rabbi)
and outside the lines of parental approval
(she and Dan eloped)

she practiced in between the lines of notes
I continue to carry the torch-
songs on the very same ivories

Kate Lamberg

'tis You, My Friend

The phrase I love you
is not needed
the syllables and rhythms
through the warmth
of your voice
mark the words that caress me,
give thoughts to reflect

In an unearthly place to
safely dwell
you pass no judgment
in my tangled search
For me, you smile
knowingly when I look
on in disbelief,
your laughter melodies
sooth my disarray.

Gentle is your touch as
your fingertips stroke my soul,
You, who feels what I see
and sees what I feel,
who speaks so quietly,
yet in volumes to me.

It is you, my friend
beautiful you.

Pd Edwards

The Write Word

As a newlywed, I cherished my close girlfriends. I learned to lean on them for all things vital in my day-to-day existence: companionship, confession, connection and counsel.

Our sisterhood expanded with our waistlines, as we welcomed babies and embraced motherhood. We filled whatever role was necessary to meet each other's needs in the moment: friend, confidante, sister or mother. We bartered our meager services: babysitting, mending, baking and carpooling. But our most valuable resources were free for the taking.

Cheer: in the face of tedium; consolation – when faced with defeat.
Humor: in the midst of tears; tears – when nothing less would do.
Praise: without envy or restraint; admonition – when nothing more was required.

But it was Mary Belle who sanded my life's hard edges.

My husband knew her first and introduced us during our early years of marriage. With her genteel manners, bright smile and gift for music, Mary Belle was easy to like. Although hundreds of miles and two states separated us, we fed our growing friendship with occasional phone calls, frequent letters and – more recently – weekly emails.

There is a peculiar intimacy that evolves through correspondence. Thoughtful words, whether penned with deliberation or scrawled in haste, are concrete. Permanent. Lasting. As lasting as sisterhood's connection. Somehow, that very knowledge adds a particular weight to the act of writing and an importance to the friendship itself. And Mary Belle is important.

For thirty-some years, she has served as both my model and my mentor. I learned from her relationships with her children, then her grandchildren. I listened to her words of experience. I trusted her advice. I grew to admire and look up to her like a wiser, older sister.

Hand-written in dainty script, her carefully worded letters crowd my desk drawers, prized for the seasons of wisdom they contain. Cherished for the decades of unconditional support they show. Valued for the lasting bond they represent.

And today, more than ever, when I count my blessings – and my sisters – Mary Belle tops the list. As well she should.

Now a vintage 94, my husband's childhood piano teacher still has lots to offer this appreciative 54-year-old!

Carol McAdoo Rehme

South-bound Soaring

Sit with me, my sisters, over hearty fist-punched
loaves and sip too many cups of sweet-pressed cider.
Taste with me tang-tart tomatoes, and help me fry
green and glorious early vine-robbed slices for supper's
homespun feast. Test with me dry vintages of summer's
choke-cherries and sample clear and sparkling pot-boiled
jelly. Chat and gaggle with me as I fashion lattice crusts
for brimming gravied pies of venison and partridge
while darkness closes prematurely in, September's
skies too early showing signs of chilly turquoise.
And learn with me the lesson taught by soaring vees of
south-bound geese: if a single wing-beat falters, all
willingly await the fallen one's rejoining that fleet flock.

Carol Knepper

Portrait of an Aunt

Aunt Mary lives in a small midwestern town
where everyone knows everyone too well
but very few know her
and that's the way she likes it

She's fastidious and frugal to a fault
washing mustard jars and soup cans
before putting them away
in her germfree cupboard

She boils up three eggs
and fools you into thinking
her egg salad is so filling
dessert would be superfluous

Aunt Mary loves quietly
from behind her faded apron
No public flaunting of affection
but you know if you are favored

Barbara Moore

Halved

Her eyes are worded cruelly,
it's in the glare; two lighthouses
flashing on a coastline face.

The left arm balancing two worlds:
holding and hiding, giving and taking,
gift, non-gift, apple, non-apple.

She queries the love of paint,
the brush, the hand, his eye,
knows it's sad and she, pitiful.

Or, maybe she doesn't think that
at all. Perhaps she's planning
a dinner for two, shocked

she's forgotten parsley, thyme.
But the snug fit of her terrier's neck
to the gap of a flicked up leg,

content on the couch as a halved peach
in a bowl full of full peaches,
makes me believe, otherwise

Jacqui Corcoran

Pieces of You

A bright day spent in the sun with blue-haired
old ladies bickering over bits of you, hungry for
a few knick-knacks to take up some space, leaving
me hollow, blind-sided by sorrow I *never* dreamed
possible when it came to you and I

Those asinine bodice busters you used to read
stacked high on the table in front of me by a lady
anxious to get to reading, damn near had me reeling
as I remembered you devour
"The Flame and The Flower"
with such *divine* anticipation

That silly red hat you found so charming?
I found it quite alarming watching a casual shopper
carelessly finger it up—
(lady get your fucking hands off my mom's hat!)
up only to toss it back onto
the table, allowing me to catch my breath

It took all I had to keep from screaming while
handing over pieces of you to strangers having
no idea what treasures they carried home

> *Memories of our lives bagged up*
> *for pennies on the dollar*
> *Lost chances and hopes going*
> *at red slashed prices …*

Our journey together is over now
There will be no resolution, no
bright new evolution of you and I

You've passed on, but life goes on with me packing
a case while trying to erase visions of a life I once knew
being carted away on a hot summer day

Pieces of me and …
               … pieces of you …

Alicia Winski

Granny

Granny had dreams.

She wanted to create paintings that took people's breath away.

She wanted to write novels that would have her readers hanging on every word.

But, in Granny's life and time, such dreams were considered sheer folly. Instead, she did what was expected of a young woman barely out of her childhood, and tucked those dreams away, storing them deep in the back of a closet where they would never see the light of day, and became a mother. Eventually, she gave life to eleven children and was the most stable, maternal figure of my early years.

In all of my memories of her, Granny wears the same faded flowered print dress, and a hand embroidered apron tied neatly around her waist. She stands at the counter of the kitchen that was the hub of the home her husband built for the family.

It wasn't a fancy house, and resembled more of a square box than anything else. Old sheets sufficed as coverings for the doors and closets. The linoleum was faded soon after it was new, worn down by eleven pairs of feet that eventually multiplied to include those of son/daughter-in-laws and countless grandchildren. What rugs there were in the house were hand-braided, sewn from scraps of clothing no longer suitable to be worn.

There wasn't much in the way of furniture, because it was a given that most everything that made its way into the house was of necessity, and absent of want. The only exception to that rule, stood in the corner of the living room, an ancient upright piano. It's keys were worn through the ivory to the wood, yet it could fill the house the most amazing honky tonk music whenever one of my uncles got the urge to sit and play it by ear.

If the furniture was sparse, the wall coverings even more so. Other than a smattering of aged photographs of relatives I never knew, there were two store bought plagues that hung on the kitchen wall. One, taking its rightful place above the long handmade bench and table that served to feed the masses, declared that *the family that prayed together, would stay together,* and the other was a much smaller framed picture of a garden, a gift from Granny's husband on an early anniversary. I can still recall the words of the poem neatly scripted amid the flowers.

I never knew, what life could hold
Of bliss beyond compare,
Until I trod loves garden
And found you walking there

Then every flower was beautiful
The lovely garden through
And life itself a lovely thing
All because of you

~Anonymous

I suppose the poem stuck with me all these years, because it was so out of place. I couldn't reconcile in my young mind anyone thinking about or talking to Granny that way. She wasn't the kind of person that anyone ever fussed over, and looking back I can't help but recollect that she was very much taken for granted.

She was a small woman, but a strong one. She was opinionated and resourceful. Some might have even referred to her as God-fearing, because she never missed a Sunday in church, but I have a feeling it might have been God that would have feared her more.

She didn't back down from anyone -- including the husband she chased with a broom when he tried to bring a case of beer into the house against her wishes, or in the face of a shotgun poised and cocked, with an irate neighbor staring down the barrel from the other end over a dispute about a blueberry patch. From my child's mind-eye perspective I'd always figured that God wouldn't have stood a chance going toe to toe with Granny.

When I was young, I learned so much from her. She passed down skills and traditions; teaching me how to bake pies from freshly picked wild berries and how to braid my own rugs. Every day after school she'd sit me down in a chair next to her rocker and patiently teach me how to purl and knit. Yet, in the same breath, she also seemed to want to see me come into my own, as she encouraged my creativity; something I suspect no one ever did for her.

Sometimes the greatest lesson we can learn from someone else, is to watch and feel the pain of their struggles with being essentially human. It was in my adult years I learned so much more from Granny, incidental lessons that changed my world. Sadly, the biggest lesson came with her passing.

Granny lived and breathed for her family. She was always there when ever anyone needed her, just as she was always there for me. It was her house that I went to when I fell ill at school, and it is her house where I remember spending holidays, eating Sunday dinners and playing on hot summer days.

But when it came time for Granny to go toe to toe with God, she went alone. Not only did she pass away in the night when no one was there, but no one knew about it for days. Despite raising almost a dozen children, no one noticed she was gone. The sadness I feel about that after all these years is still palatable.

When I think of her now, I put myself in a faded floral print dress, with a neatly tied apron around my waist. I think of spending my entire day making one meal after another for sometimes up to 25 people at a time, day after day; with no complaints, no expectations of recognition in return. And I think of dying alone with dreams tucked away deep in the back of a closet never to see the light of day.

You see, I have dreams too.

I want to create paintings that take someone's breath away.

I want to write a novel that will have my readers hanging on every word.

And yet, I want to be there for my family. I want my grandchildren to think of me when they remember hot summer days and Sunday dinners.

I want it all.

With her passing Granny taught me life's biggest lesson - that no one should give up their dreams simply because they become a parent, and that although motherhood is an honorable role, it isn't the entire person. Now I think of her as human, with hopes and dreams unmet, pushed aside for sacrifice and a greater good, yes - but if she had been born in a different time, maybe she too, could have had it all.

Kimberley Rockdale

She Knows a Recipe for Jam

How to pick the plum one,
how to wash and prepare the skin,
to flash boil and peel,
to dig meaty pulp,
and mash the flesh.

I want her
when I watch her hands
slice and dice
the fruit—
plums, pears, apples.

The sweet soul of each
waits for her hands.
I am only lemon
the sour juice
without sugar.

She turns my skin
tangerine.

There's just enough sweetness
to bring her back
to peel the thick layers
covering me.

When I argue that this can't last
she reveals a recipe
to preserve this delicacy.

Trish Falin

Family Reunion

No one knows
what to say to me
least of all
the cousins
who all married
high school boys
after graduation

Their lives are
children-filled
They think it odd
that I have none
I am the childless freak
with the same boyfriend
for over 20 years

They are on
second husbands
One is on her third
This one breaks the silence
"What's your story?"
she asks me, frowning
"Couldn't you ever commit?

Barbara Moore

The Empty Women

With all they love stripped from them,
they are, the empty women:

They stare through frozen tears that climb
and claw at a door that has no key.
They peer through the ageless windows of time
with wounded heart, on bended knee.
Submerged in an icy cold prison of water
they peer up through a slick muddy surface;
these children of a lost god's daughter
chiseling sins on oblivion's face.
Staring through shafts of sunlight waxing hotter.
Stabbing through icy veins deeper each minute.
Life's kinder to those who walk on the water,
not for those orphans who reside within it.

The empty women stare hopelessly, silently
at the rough path ahead, and a mountain too steep.
Wringing the hands and hearts ever so violently
Knowing no escape from this prison cell keep.
Children of brutality, pain, tears and death's song.
Pity them their journey for they were not warned
of the perilous path they were forced to walk on,
Clad only in old slippers worn out and torn;
on dangerous ground by life thrown and tossed;
with numb, bleeding feet they walk, then they crawl,
not realizing just how much they've lost;
unable to measure the depth of their fall.
Beneath the pounding of their heartbeats
the rain is streaking old sundowns anew.
The clouds in the sky, are tattered white sheets
hiding the whisper of soft cobalt blue.
This winter beach is strewn with broken sea shells
washed up by a jigsaw puzzle ocean

That whispers of dark secrets but never tells
of broken vows and tarnished devotion.
Stars fall from their black velour mantle above
burning to cinders in the ashtray of night.
Invisible now, erased by dawn's wet glove,
the wounded elegy of broken moonlight.
Clinging to the past they've become as such,
empty women crying in desperation;
Hungering in the dark for a quicksilver touch;
finding no hope, no consolation.
A cold finger infused with blood red ink
scrawls across this tear stained remnant
of hope that was lost in a wink, in a blink.
A story too forlorn to ever recant

Empty women, past the point of return,
twisting inside the cocoon of death's kiss.
These butterflies were born, only to burn,
in this moment that never was, but always is.
These women trapped in a nightmarish dream;
invisible women, hearts cracked at the mast;
these empty women are the last primal scream,
still hanging on to the invisible past.

With all they love stripped from them,
        they are.....
                the empty women.

Candice James

Wild Ponies/Women in Chains

(Wild Ponies)

thunder resonates within slender cages carved of bone;
sounds reminiscent of the hard hammering of hooves bruising
the tender terrain of free spirits in flight, lassoed with
enticing, soothing reassurances of quieting, gentle hands

warm pulsations flowing feverishly through subterranean rivers
exhaling apprehension with each heaving breath, captive fillies
softly eased into confining corrals built high with slats of domesticity
painted in neutral, mute colors of safety and security

(Women in Chains)

futilely chafing against bits and bridles persuasively thrust between
clenched teeth of resistance; shod in Versace and shackled by golden
Gucci tethers tarnished with time, tempestuous natures are reined in by
deceptively delicate links heavy as lead, formed and forged in despair

>   *seamlessly welded by*
>   *the passing of years and loss of self*

saddled by predisposition, broken under weighty responsibility,
eventuality finds them discontentedly grazing in fields of middle-aged
sensibilities and middle-class moralities, bitterly digesting dry dreams
and longings for lost youth unbound by chains and
>   *wild ponies running free*

for the wild ponies in my life, may we always run free...

Alicia Winski

Division of Sound vs Matter

While I may not be great at math
I do know the value of a true friend.

Folds of femininity
tease the crux of Cupid's
sordid fairy tale

Mathematics in my mind
are misgiving and unkind

I must recalculate.

Apryl Skies

American Beauty

Girl-next-door
bodacious brunette
doe-like eyes
sweet, sensuous smile
crowned one night
before her time.

Sun-bleached blonde
wisps of gold frame face
painted and shimmered
conceals resignation
dream of future
of body, not mind.

American Beauty
held in high-esteem
jealous gazes abound
façade of friends
one-night-stands line the wall
like the trophy you are.

Time comes to pass
What to show for it all?
swinging down poles
dollar bills on the floor
or give up on life
obey, plastic wife

Still, an American doll.

Amanda LaPera

Porn ☆

I came across a porn site last night
searching for erotic music to highlight
my sensual musings--
You know
the kind of writing
screaming for hypnotic middle-eastern music
designed to seduce foolish men into
opening up their wallets to practiced pretties

    love me, fuck me
as though they were one and the same,

purchasing sexuality and desires
for love sensuously expressed
in brown-paper-wrapped murmurings--

    don't hurt me, love me
as though they are not one and the same,
        as they are one and the same

I hadn't seen porn since I was young
I didn't care for it then;
        I don't much care for it now;
cold, corporate manufactured intimacy
between desperate men and women

no, that's not love,
        that's not even good sex

but my attention was caught and fascinated,
I watched it for a while enthralled
by the raw moaning and groaning
of a woman on the screen;

a tired bleached blonde
perched on hands and knees,
wearing cheap spiked heels
and cheesy thigh-highs, growling,
>   *hurt me, fuck me*

her pale sex-slick skin jiggling
with every monotonous thrust against it,
>   *hurt me, fuck me*

>   *as though they were one and the same,*
>   *as they are one and the same*

. . . and I wondered,
>   *Who's more honest between she and I?*

We're both porn stars--
>   *She fucks for money,*
>   *I fuck for love*

Pondering these thoughts
I sat drinking my luke-warm coffee,
mesmerized by a bird throwing itself against
my window, screaming, cawing,
wings flapping frantically against glass
as he tried desperately to break through my solitude,
eventually killing himself in the process

I felt badly…

Maybe I should have let him in,
but I didn't know
if he wanted to love me or fuck me

Then again, aren't they one and the same?

Alicia Winski

Porno Woman

Hey porno women: I blame you because it started
when I found your gloss in the green trunk as I squatted
on the damp, unfinished cellar floor.

My rusty hammer slammed one-two-three,
and the padlock released. I listened for the hum
of Mom's blue Dodge Dart, pushed squeaky lid up to see,
stacks of you, locked away safe like a gun
in a metal box. Naked with pigtails and lollipops.
This is what Daddy likes: round hard asses, perky breasts.

This is what Daddy likes.

I carry a pile of you up black plastic-lined stairs, and hide you
on top shelf of my closet so I can study you, day and night.
Thin white skin spread, open and tight and round and pinks,
reds, wet lips and mouths hanging wide in — *oh, oh, ohs.*

A brunette in felt hat straddles an old rusty bike
on a farm; she has no hair where even I now grow it.
You alone I love and you I forgive because you can't know
who I am or that I'm only twelve and shouldn't have to see you
or your naked friends.
You are like a younger sister and I keep you safe
when I gaze into your lusty eyes, so much like mine.

But I am not beautiful like you, paper dolls. I'm weak;
I'm fat. I hate myself with every fiber of my being.
This full-length mirror enlarges every bulge, every blossom,
every non-skinny, fat ass part of me.

I hate your 92 pounds from every angle. Lying in bed later,
I'll be counting my ribs.

1…I want no breasts
2…I want no hips
3…I want no

No, no, no—
to be a porno woman loved by you.

Sheila Hageman

Happy V Day

I. The Wedding Party

I was invited to a friend's wedding party, who thought it would be kitch to have it on Valentine's Day. I chose to be depressed that particular Valentine's day, for no *specific* reason. I just wanted to take it in a different direction that year. A direction I later seriously regretted. I showed up at the party, I mean wedding thingy, fashionably late (three hours) in my cute cocktail dress and my recycled gift – a porcelain pineapple chatchke which said "Have a great day!" on the top.

I engaged in idle conversation with horridly boring people while I picked the frosting off of the vegan wedding cake and was waiting for an opportune moment to grab the little edible groom figure off the top. Suddenly there was a tap on my shoulder.

"Are you Camille?" The girl looked at me in a strangely familiar way. "I'm Liz." She said.

She didn't even glance at my plate. Okay, I wasn't in trouble for eating the groom. No. No. No. It was far, far worse.

"Didn't you date Steve Gumbaronni?" She asked.

Dating, hmm…such a loose term, I thought to myself, did we "date"? I guess that could qualify. He helped me move some boxes out of my garage when I was moving and I gave him the last five seasons of The Jefferson's DVD set in exchange for his labor, which lead into that loosely termed word, "dating".

"Yeah, I did briefly date Steve, why?" I replied.

She looked to her friend who stood next to her with a smug look on her face…a fat smug look on her face. Okay, I guess a look can't be fat, but she *was* fat. And if she was a nice person, I wouldn't call her fat at all. I'd call her chubby, or full-figured, or fresh-face farm girl from the Mid West. The skinny girl Liz, with the bad skin continued…

"Did you wear protection?"

My heart started pounding.

"What do you mean?" I asked.

She looked back at her friend, who had become increasingly fat to me because of her bad attitude. Bad skin Liz who, by the way, was flat-chested, got more and more flat-chested and more and more blemished as she spoke, because she too was a bitch, carried on…

"He gave me venereal warts."

Her now obese friend, nodded in an almost pleasurable agreement. Pock Mark and The Whale stood there for a moment, yearning for a dramatic response from me. I wasn't gonna give it to them, I wasn't going to play their reindeer games - I was gonna play it real cool.

"That's awful, I am really sorry to hear that." I said.

Nemo finally piped in, obviously unsatisfied with my performance.

"I heard that sometimes the warts are so far up in you, you'd never know you had them, until you die of ovarian cancer. C'mon Liz, let's eat cake."

The grim sex reapers took off – leaving me with the gimped-groom, and a possible disease.

II. - Planned Parenthood Santa Monica

It was an early morning at Planned Parenthood Santa Monica – the quickest appointment I could get, in the least ghetto neighborhood I could find – for free women's healthcare – (God bless America…) I had hoped that it would be an up-grade from the period stained waiting chairs at the Hollywood Branch – but I guess they too shared the same designer. I sat in the waiting room for a while catching up on the latest STD literature. Fascinating.

Several young Latino women sat there, some with boyfriends, some alone. I stopped reading the pamphlets, it was making me too paranoid and decided to play abortion roulette instead – with the girls in the waiting room as I mentally called them out as I saw it…Abortion. Abortion. V.D. Check-up. Herpes. Abortion. Pap smear. Pill re-fill. Abortion. Suddenly, an echoing voice came out of the loud speaker.

"Ms. Solari, you're next."

It was like I was in Vagina Purgatory and finally the Arch Angel swept down to get me.

A skinny white girl with gorgeous acrylic nails escorted me to the doctor's room and handed me the paper nighty, then left. I took my clothes off and set them neatly aside. Then I put on the paper nighty, which seemed like the same material as the lobster smocks we would wear when my father took the family out for "Lobstah rolls" in The Cape. Back then my sister and I would grab the fresh lobsters from the tank in the front of the restaurant and have lobster drag races.

After a long wait, a large African American women in a white coat walked in wearing rubber gloves.

"Now, how are we doing today little one?" She asked in a heavy southern drawl.

I thought about how much vagina she must have seen today

already and how she has such a good attitude about it.

"I'm okay." I said.

"Now, you here for a check-up, is that right?" She asked.

I paused, embarrassed.

"Well actually I came to see if I have... (mumbling) *unexpected friends*?"

"What?" She asked.

"I said. I came to see if...there was anything *going on down there.*"

The Doctor now stern; "Honey, just spit it out, I found a Tonka truck up a girls vagina once, ain't nothing you say could surprise me." She replied.

I took a deep breath and said it with clarity this time. "Wanna make sure I don't have venereal warts." *Yuck! I said that horrible word – veneeeeereal...*

I waited for a disapproving response from her, but instead, this absolute angelic woman was like a tour guide at Disney World – explaining how to get on the ride.

"Alright darling, we'll check it out - you know the drill, put your little feet in the stirrups and lean back. C'mon don't be shy, pull yourself forward a bit, that's right, that's right, now keep your hands next to you and hold tight...."

She began to inspect the goods. I was scared, it was scary, she wasn't saying anything, was she holding back? Was she so mortified that she didn't know how to phrase it...was there a Tonka truck in my vagina?

Suddenly she spoke. "Alright honey, we're all set here."

"Is everything alright?" I asked nervously.

She paused for a moment taking a deep breath.

"God gave you some beautiful eyes, but he gave you a fucked up vagina... I'll be right back, we gonna have ourselves a little talk."

What did she mean? How was it fucked up? And how come Doctor Villafranca the family doctor growing up never pointed out that I had some kind of a problem down there? Was it a new problem? Was it an old problem? Was the problem that Doctor Villafranca always referred to my vagina as a "bum bum".

I passed out.

Then, I woke up to a large woman holding a mirror to my...*stuff.*

"Well don't you wanna know why your vagina's fucked up?" She asked.

"Do I have a disease? I replied.

"First of all, I want to point something out here (holding up the mirror to my "bum bum") You see, when you got one brother on one side and another brother on the other side, you're okay" She explained.

"Okay. I don't really know what that means, but do I have a disease?" I asked again.

She chuckled. "Oh honey, you got no diseases, but you do have a tilted uterus. It means when you have sex, you gotta do it doggy-style so it don't hurt. I'll show you a picture."

"No. no. no, that's okay…. I know what that is… well okay… you can show me a picture if you want."

She began to show me pictures of sex positions that would hurt and what positions were more desirable. I admired her. I liked that she liked her job. But moreover… I liked the fact that I was disease free.

Happy V Day America.

Love,
Camille

Thorna Eldritch: Shadow of a Self-Portrait

The sky burns azure
the breeze breathes brisk
wish this warlock
weather
would whisk-whisk-whisk
me away
from the everyday
tsk tsk tsk
and the twin doppelgangers
of pain and risk
(they see with cloudy-eyed clarity)
~~   ~~   ~~   ~~   ~~   ~~

If only his member
were an obelisk
to which she could pray...
ejecta to wash
the reaching
tree-arms away
...from her snowpure
sepulchered
canvas

Gloria J. Wimberley

That Hot Afternoon

When the electricity shut off
only dogs barked
and you stood on the balcony
silently watching me undress,
smoking a cigarette.

Workers blocked a street
to repair a broken pole
while I picked out a bra
and you tucked hair behind an ear.
My eyes caught your unguarded stare
of skin covered with sweat.

Later I might argue that you
were longing in the quiet hour
for television, a radio, that no one
was home from work to talk about the day.

And I might say later that you were lovely
or just that you had black hair
pulled back off your shoulders
with eyes empty on a clear day.

Trish Falin

Like God

Sunlight takes eight minutes to illuminate her wares
the picnic basket she carries around between her legs
a moveable feast
invariably consumed on unconsecrated ground
I'm a combine harvester
she's the pasture I get to thresh

between the light & first sight
at the melt point of inhibition
her chapel of rest eclipses the sun
she becomes my valkyrie
I am her slain, she has the hoodoo buju over me
I am inert under her
a toxic gas mattress

decanting can take some time
a smooth white leg accelerates matters
connection dilates
focuses my pin pricked mind
on the goose steps to heaven
theology collapses/art relapses/enter synopsis

re-created as a synthetic synthesis
aided & abetted by the radiant energy
emitted from her bejeweled trap
the geyser sings a lullaby

I see boudicca on her chariot
a walking prism of predilections
straddling rays of light
solar powering her own internal combustion

I'm a sputnik
riding the rocket
going vertical
toward the glowing red alumni

Like God, only…

only wiser
only quicker
only whiter
only sexier

only more debased
more tuned in
more moreish
like god, only…
better.

Teri Louise Kelly

Dark Muse

Can't stop reminiscing – the hair that embraced you –
brown satin flesh –
breasts holding firm above mine –
our skin was stretched so tightly
there was no blood to run through us –
only heat lived
and made its way coarsely, thudding violently
over our arms –
my legs were wet
dampened by the confrontation.

No sudden thought before
collapsing into your skin; breasts holding –
solid buds of enveloped pleasure.
How I wanted you – your violence
laid down to my desire – where I topped you,
held you against a street rail,
winding my legs across yours to feel the moistness you carried.
I think I may have known you before,
but for now
this is haunting...

Jessica Wilson

Night Fever
For my friend, Meg

The dark tongues of night's dogs
lick at our ankles. We crave wine, endless talk,

irony followed by uncertain laughter.
We find our place at the bar,

ask for Bloody Marys and fish tacos.
You flash white teeth in response

to the blonde woman who stares
at you as if your breasts were cupcakes.

How I love these times…
They are what has become of my shy silences.

I know what grief your eyes have seen.
You've eaten dahlias and carried old loves

in the small purse at your side.
Years of light and dark shiver behind us. We both wear

silver, mind our manners. You are my heart's friend,
the ringing of a bell in this peculiar temple.

Martina Reisz Newberry

To Heather after Nine Years of Friendship

We were best friends –sitting there
in the sand. Our arms
washed up on our laps, as we looked
at each other, we knew
our moment
would never last.

Jessica Wilson

As Girlfriends Do

I thought of you at this moment…
I rarely do, I have better things to
tend to now.
We were notorious young ingénue
outlaws, we played a mean game of
Scrabble remember? Inviting boys over
for some *wordplay*.
Shooting pool at The Corner Pocket on
Sunset Blvd. Carousing with the best
and the worst of them. The riff- raff
misfits and renegades.
I found a way to misfit in.
I liked when you played your piano and sang
"Desperado" it was sad and lovely
and sad.
We had lots of loaded fun before you would
turn into 'Ms. Hyde' about twice a week, it
got to be, before your hateful
hissing venom spitting fork tongue
bit me through the slow gin fizzes.
We laughed and gorged and purged
up a thunderstorm. Flailing across country
in a black-out, landing in a jail cell in Banning.
You drove. You were always in the driver seat.
I rode shotgun and handed you my I.D.
I hated loving you, my wildebeest
bad girl, partner in 'drama queen' crime.
Try saying that 3 times sober…
Our tiaras tilted, our crowns cut like
thorns on roses.
We bled
together
as girlfriends do.

L.K. Thayer

Second Chance

The woman in the shop watches me with a sympathetic smile. She sees how unhappy I am, how every shirt or skirt I hold in front of me makes my frown deepen while I turn this way and that, finally giving up and returning the items to their hangers. Nothing about me is right anymore.

"Can I help you?" I didn't notice her moving towards me, but there she is, smiling that same smile, offering me help.

I laugh. "I doubt it, not unless you can do plastic surgery and have a side-line as a beautician and hairdresser."

Her smile doesn't falter. "Follow me. There's something I think you should see."

I hesitate, but she has marched off ahead of me, and something about her makes me feel I have to follow. She stops outside the fitting rooms, pulls back a curtain and signals for me to enter.

"I've left something in there for you. Try it on, see how it feels, and if you like it, you can keep it – no charge."

I start to speak, but with a gentle hand in the small of my back she has pushed me into the cubicle and let the curtain fall to hide me from the rest of the world. At first I can't make out what the thing is that hangs on the wall, then I realise it's another skin. I shudder at the thought of trying it on. Where the hell did it come from? I reach for the curtain, but the woman pokes her head in and smiles and nods. She's creeping me out as much as the skin and I feel I have to do what she says or my own skin might end up in one of these rooms.

I take the skin down from the hook. At first it doesn't feel like it will fit, but I wriggle a little and it's as though every pore, every hair follicle, every crease has to match up with the template beneath. I avoid looking in the mirror while this process is taking place; it feels clammy at first and I'm sure that if I look I will see a snake like apparition staring back. I know that snakes aren't clammy; we all know that snakes aren't clammy – but that's not what our eyes tell us.

Slowly I raise my eyes and look into the full-length mirror. I'm surprised to see that this transformation, which felt so radical, is simply a different version of me. I hoped I would see a 6ft tall athletic male and find out how different we really are, or a ninety year old woman with great wisdom to impart – maybe even a child with years of life in credit. But no – it's just me.

Then I look closer; it's an improved version of me. There are no stretch marks, no wrinkles, no worry lines. I have a golden tan, soft, silken skin – I have shed my eczema, my psoriasis, my acne; I haven't had skin like this since I was twelve years old. My muscles are toned, my teeth are white and even and I get the impression that I'm a couple of inches taller.

I run my fingers along my arm and revel in the smoothness. My legs, too, feel like an advert for hair depilatories, impossibly silky shiny. I go closer to the mirror and look into my eyes; the whites are so bright, the blue so clear, as though they have never seen horror, never felt pain, never told a lie. Never lived a life.

Is it worth it then? If I swap my real body, the one that shows in its scars and its wrinkles, in its aches and in its pains, a life lived to the full, a life of experience – if I swap it for this perfect version, untouched by the real world, will I only be left with a shell? With an empty, barren husk?

I smile my beautiful smile, throw back my glossy hair and watch it caress my perfect, golden shoulders. I let my hands play softly on the just visible rib-cage and snake past the slender hips. I give my unreachable self a little wave and undo the zip. What I have may not be perfect but it's the real me. We've been through a lot together, me and my skin; I wouldn't have it any other way.

As I leave the shop the woman who served me is nowhere to be seen. Somehow I'm not surprised.

Ma Ze

"**Ma** ze wintery wintery"
the saleswoman yelled
when I gave her a reason
for not buying her 800 shekel Paris dress.
"Ma ze ma ze?
Ze lo beseder geveret
ha hatoona b'yuni,"
She pulled my sleeves and poked
to no avail,
I couldn't've bought her dress even if I liked it.

ma ze – what's this?
Ze lo beseder geveret – that's not good lady
ha hatoona b'yuni, - the wedding is in June

Lois Michal Unger
97

Birthday Lunch Autopsy

Three hours of adding insult to injury on every topic had shredded my last nerve. Surrounded by shopping bags, we were sharing a birthday lunch in a Ruby Tuesday bar booth, my companion under the influence of a pharmaceutical with a consonant laden name I hadn't retained. Her twitchy energy was a dead giveaway, I remember that well enough.

My appetizer arrived first and her fork rocketed toward it, snagging a healthy chunk of crab cake. "Hey, this is all I'm having. I'd like to have it," I said, contemplating my own launch across the table to pop her a good one – a couple more loose marbles weren't going to make much of a difference either way.

My sullenness didn't appear to register, and I was a fool for holding my tongue for so long just to save my own skin, and maybe fearing volatile reaction made me a wimp enabler, but I was a mouse trapped in a maze. I either let the day grind to its expected end or pay a fifty mile cab fare home. Guilt was the weapon of choice, how she continually roped me into these things. My benevolence, though waning, hammered the final nail in the coffin each time.

She'd rung me dry ragging on every person ever met before gunning for total strangers – a quick-draw artist with killer aim at every schmuck having drawn breath in her general vicinity since she beamed down to Earth.

"Is it white-trash day at Macy's?

"They sell mirrors upstairs, lady. Do us a favor and buy one.

"There should be a law against men *that* ugly. Kiss a porker, win a prize."

Eyes closed and chewing my jacked crab cake, she moaned as though Fabio were sucking her big toe. I'd heard the meds accelerate appetite. If nothing else, the side effects were kicking in. Her doctor couldn't possibly know the whole story, was surely laboring under symptom misdirection. It's one thing to profess depression between sobs, and another to admit utter despise. Nonetheless, I repeatedly proved to be one who mutely take notes rather than openly question, or god forbid, contradict her behavior – give me a half-hour with her doc and he'd change his tune to antisocial personality disorder. For starters.

And yes, circumstance didn't cut her the best break. But instead of taking the high road, she sank into conspicuous psychosis. Some rungs south of saintly myself, I'll throw only a few stones. From where I sat watching the woman chowing on my lunch, she was in deeper than I had rope length to rescue her.

From way back, Miss Dilettante thought highly of herself. Adamant she suffered a secondhand childhood, and martyrdom since, she concocted an alternate persona. Not one flew over the cuckoo's nest crazy, more the ragged edge of deceptive practices. But then, I'm no licensed expert. I was twenty the first time I witnessed the transformation – most pronounced when unveiled for the opposite sex – and I was sufficiently startled. For all his thespian skill, Jack Nicholson had nothing on her.

A counterfeit smile rose amid sour demeanor even an icing of L'Oréal couldn't sweeten. When a seven year relationship ended abruptly, I felt bad and commiserated. Yet, I'd been confidant to how she hated all near and about the man except for his boyfriend status. The self-preserving bastard fled the scene the night he met someone new. I certainly couldn't fault the bastard for long.

I encouraged her to join social networking and connect with former high school friends. "Meet some new people," I said. "It's fun." And although she didn't know anyone from high school she cared for a second connection with, she joined to leave in a fury after a few short months. The pressure to *like* on a routine basis wasn't her cup of arsenic; her last post collectively referred to unknown residents of her town as boozers and breeders. She claimed it was a joke.

"When I'm good, I'm very good. When I'm bad, I'm better." Trying to exude prevalence, a screwy superior gaze greeted the masses, men and women, friends and foes. If she had been an authentic starlet she might have worked the script to her advantage, but Mae West she wasn't. The word "sham" always came to mind.

More than one male acquisition was paraded before me and my husband. We served as smoke screen to introduce a semblance of normalcy by proximity. Sadly, each time this magician's trick was ruined by clumsy execution using a favored, original quote: "I call my daughter 'Air Jordan' because she has nothing between her ears but air." I flinched on her behalf while she glowed at the wisecrack because I knew any dating prospect ended in that instant. Her best talent lay not in persuading a participant onto the stage, but in making him vanish in a puff of smoke. Abracadabra.

Efforts to sway her from unsuitable options on our last birthday shopping trip bombed as she cooed over The Limited fashions thirty years her junior – circling and pulling the sequin-studded, boob-baring separates from brimming racks. "Oh, isn't this cute," she said in a dilated-pupil-blurred reality. I buttoned my lips, counting the minutes until she wound down and the birthday obligation finished. Not that my presence counted for more than an optical illusion masking self-imposed ostracization.

And even my charity expired when I found I was on her blacklist alongside the other schmucks, learned how she enthusiastically defamed me too. Turns out I'm a hillbilly from the sticks; an untrustworthy fake who believes I live a perfect life; the hack who merely imagines I can write, who in grand delusion pays editors to publish in their journals. Wouldn't you know, upon dissection she labeled me the confused sham.

At best, my sister is a politically incorrect cynic who can't see the forest while leveling every last tree. At worst, a Picasso image trapped alone inside a carnival mirror.

Bella

Always the awkward feather
brushed away as nuisance,
e(strange)d to the world

comfortable among
broken pottery & one-eyed orphans
safe among hazard signs

lost in the crowd
small like Alice in mirrored reflection
the ugly duckling, before the swan

Always trying too hard
or not enough, a voice
frail against the song of youth

the tired truth of experience
silenced by cold hands
and impatient tongues

Bella was forever
Mrs. Peacock in the library,

~rope in hand~

hanging on harsh words.

She Sits on the Landing

She sits on the landing
next to the bedroom
at the top of the stairs.
Though the door is closed,
she hears everything.
Every complaint about her:
her laziness, her messiness,
her thin skin...how the woman
behind the door has read her diary
that was stashed under her mattress.
When she hears the phone click,
she races down the stairs
to her room, shuts the door.
Resolves she will never open it
to anyone.

Melissa Grossman

The Master

I was weeping when I met her
helpless exhaustion
took hold and would not
release its grip

She did nothing
but sit with me
as I spent my tears
in 5's and 10's
even in her silence
she was fully present

I told her that now
was not a good time
to spread my wings
with all that transpired
I feared I would not
have the strength

She told me I was at
an impasse in my life
a crossroads
my decision
would make all the difference
I could not help
those around me if
I neglected myself

The time for growth
was present
if I didn't take this step
I would not fully
understand the lesson

Her words felt like
soothing electric blue waves
washing over the maroon
of my frustrations

Her eyes danced with compassion
and a trustful knowing
that was free from the hues
of arrogance

I wanted to lean
into her comfort
understand the depths
of her sureness
and wrap my arms
around her words

"What we do today
will affect seven generations"

So I stepped into
the sacred circle
and became her
humble student

Tracie Skarbo

The Pen & The Pearl
For Alicia, Cklara, Gloria & Pearl S. Buck

She dreams, she dreams…

Silk slippers await her feet
for her to slink away into twilight
upon cold floors, descending downward
into friendly black hours
when it is quiet, it is quiet here
in these dark-muse corners
where the moon is her only witness
until dawn paws cat-like
cracking the fragile morning wide open
silence, sage in its slumber.

Ink drips from dry fingers
She is the howl of the voiceless
devouring silence onto parchment
into the psyche, into history
chains of the enslaved loosen their grip
to her words--
she listens and absorbs the crying wind and walls
walls of oppression and injustice
burst like the sun,

Her wisdom;
a shelter from the storm outside her
outside her frailty, sensibility and belief
beyond a hope she harbors
no demise.

Somehow in this moment, she is a touch away
a touch away from god
a touch away from truth
closer to the sublime mystery within her
a paradox which curses all she has been taught
no matter

Somehow in this moment there is no time
only movement of hand
the curved landscape of sound
scratching upon flattened white textures,
heavy, stacked like stones

Sea birds soar from shore
and for a moment the ocean roars
in acknowledgment of her finality
in this moment, in this cold, dark corner
hovering above these floor-panels
in her silk slipper silence
the Pearl glimmers immortality.

She lives, she lives…

To You, Anaïs

Anaïs,
I attempt to write to you, the old fashioned way
as if my #2 pencil and crumbled up, coffee stained, lined paper
can somehow bring me closer
to your world of last century bohemian, Parisian cafés
and compulsive diary compositions and raw confessions.

Anaïs,
I waited until the last minute tonight,
to pour this out,
for I knew that after another pause,
the doubt would creep back in
and I'd never even get this far.

Anaïs,
If I had a chance to edit and scrutinize,
if Microsoft Word spell checks my shaky handwriting,
fear would set back in,
and I'd never get this far.

Anaïs,
I have a desperate desire to quote you,
to condemn this poem to the same trash piles
of school application prompts,
and my desperate desire desperately wins over my self-respect,
so I give in:

"Life shrinks or expands in proportion to our courage." you said, Anaïs.

And I have etched those words in my mind like holy words
repeated them and repeated them and repeated them
and now they are tattooed upon my skin Anaïs.

Anaïs,
When I was afraid, shrinking and shriveling into a dried apple core
I read your words aloud and planted them in my core,
grew and grew and expanded exponentially
and one day I will engrave them on my grave Anaïs.

Anaïs,
I read you out loud and courage grew in me
but I am confused.
You wrote in your diary of 1932,
that you woke up next to your oblivious husband,
took a taxi to your therapist, seduced him
so disarmed, he fucked you on his desk that day Anaïs.

You walked triumphantly to Henry Miller's shack,
took him in your delicate mouth, the twinkle in your eyes
making him defenseless Anaïs.
You fondled beautiful June, Henry's wife, on your way back,
hidden from the shame of the world by the taxi walls Anaïs.
And you were received by your cousin's charm,
then fell asleep in your husband's arms again Anaïs.

You said you felt "rich!"
You said there was enough love in you for all of them and more.
You said there was enough room in your womb for the whole world to
be engulfed.

But Anaïs,
I wonder, why was there no one to hold and engulf your tears that
night Anaïs?

Anaïs,
In all of your extravagant eroticisms,
in all of your orgies,
in the heat of sex with all the men and women,
throughout all the years with Henry,
there was so much chaos in you Anaïs.

Why were you so lonely?

Anaïs,
you wrote such raw poetry, you helped us
"open Pandora's Box, for which man's words were inadequate,"
you found the Delta of Venus for others,
but Anaïs, why did you never find your own?

Anaïs,
It takes courage to heal a broken child.
It takes courage to heal the little girl inside.
The one raped, manipulated, betrayed, abandoned,
torn and cast away, Anaïs.

I know it takes courage to trust again.

I know Anaïs.

Your father gave you your last name, Ms. Nin,
but that wasn't the only thing you didn't have a choice in.

Anaïs,
I know it takes courage to overcome,
incest burns.
It takes courage to face the truth
and strength not to fall apart between such wounds.

Anaïs,
We are not born women; we become one
and not by taking men into our wombs,
but by loving the little girl within
who needs to be born again to feel whole Anaïs.

Anaïs,
Tonight I read from the pages of your diary
and wished I could touch your bruised skin Anaïs.

Tonight I dreamt of holding your confused soul
you, with your lies and your perceived truths,
you, who can't tell pain and passion apart Anaïs.
I saw through your sad smiles
and I wanted to reach to kiss you, all of you,
hold your head to rest on my thighs Anaïs.

Incest burns Anaïs.

I know,
for I've been torn too, Anaïs.
Burned.
Not by the fire ignited
through the passion of a beautiful union
but by sin.

Anaïs, the little girl in us,
so tied to our Catholic guilt,
can only find salvation in these written confessions,
and we need courage to grow up Anaïs…

Cklara Moradian

A Kidnap
for Mina Loy

Sunk into the English hole
the earth craved her light,

but with a mind outlined in chalk,
(big dry circle)

the body became unnecessary,
a thick blackness
that would not lift,
would not storm the center.

Inside the vacuum,
her art was never given as peace.

Shrunken low and forgotten,
her words created only ghost forms
in white halls,

and music was not sound,
but a sense that rode
the crest of what was once human.

In this pale severing
without the rain,
without the stirring of limbs,
without shriek in ecstasy,
without birth or atonement,
without a murmur from the loud mass,
she was given only a stack of spheres
meant for a grave.

This was a kidnap of being,
a break in humanity,
an infertile cry for loss,
for now the woman, gone,
resists color.

In death, she was never.

April Michelle Bratten

Edna St. Vincent Millay's Apartment
For Edna

I know I'd feel right
at home; I'd lie down
on your chenille bed spread
sinking into a plucked poem

as you did, figs raw
cut open to expose
sweet female central
freshly brought in

from the Asian grocer, just below;
your hard floor to whisper ceiling windows,
with cut flowers of purple, blues, yellows-
arranged disobediently,

wearing red Chinese slippers,
you sneer at the news, finding ideas
on your fire escape, a view
only you share with pigeons

who know your brave baring-
the black and white and black
you wear to dine on leaves, rich soil;
cardinals keep for centuries behind glass,

as yellow butterflies pinned
at high school prom fly
to the steep le chase-
far from the fashionable

yet you gleam, currently
the rage; a feathered hat signals
you've been picked to write; purely
write the night and day away, wearing

the soles of those burnished Asian slippers
down a rose bower:
in a life time, disguised as an hour;
you're a shower of rubies,

colored planets that land
only to sit and write
all night, and into green goddess
dawn's hour

your piccolo cleanly sweeps
away all unnecessary verbiage;
a bit of gold mica shines
in the never ending doorways,

worshipping your abilities to say
what pops corn without electricity
what glows in the dark
without being exposed to nuclear energy

what leaves men, women, children
cats rabbits dogs deer, still in their tunneled vision

hitchhiking your beauty
from riding boot
to rainbowed heart
to dark sun out

your illumination
shall not be blown away
it was written in the
holy book of love

once lit
you live through
the purple flame
of St. Germaine

Kate Lamberg

A Conversation with a Dying Romantic

I am sorry that you are dying.
No, forgive me - do not think I will remain sad
until your bones grow cold.

You are soft and round,
you love the way a man cannot;
from the womb.

He only begs your hands and your dress.

See him not with your eyes,
but feel him with your legs.
Think as he thinks, but do not lie limp
across his bed,

as your eyes are not meant for weeping,
your heart not meant for him to record
his own darkness into.

After all, you are a woman (untame)d

Stephanie Bryant Anderson

A Scarcity of Lazarus, Who is She?
for Anna Kavan

H'Anna K floats in the translucent green glass of the bottle, carefully placed on the dressing table. She is as beautiful as ever. Her skin is whiter than my first day at school, whiter than the dentist's chair, whiter than scalpel of a surgeon cutting my legs to separate the red Orinoco from the dirt of wounds, the crucifixion of childhood; although H-Anna whispers "We were Never Never children! You and I!" she winks at me, her eyes swallow the Sun; they swallow the cats from all over London.

We go to her garden, it is overgrown like mine should be, the rain comes down at it hard, but as for us, it does not touch our skin at all, the polluted water avoids us like the plague. Before we dripped into the jungle of the city, she sunk her bazooka right into her fragile air. I felt the vapours, it was enough for everything to remain bitten by the colours that it was born in before the Eden fuck up. She folds and straightens her skirt carefully, sits delicately on the lilac painted bench. I cut some flowers for magic show later, now they bite my nails, the tendrils of the flowers grip on vowels of broken languages in the high pitch, their French manicure will cost me ten of my lives, but I don't care. The machine in a hat and an elegantly woven rope around the thick neck, the machine with the set of blazing teeth in a wide grin, the giant of ten stun grenade arms is at work in the City of London. It's counting the hair of the slaves, who will not remember their names, or their children, they'll only move their arms up and down in a slow mesmerising motion. It will not bother us here. We talk of careful slicing of silences, those that no tongue has dared to shape.

It grows dark; H'Anna K takes the umbrella folded underneath the decaying wood, upon that tight rope we walk back to the house. That customised house with amnesia of elephants in its belly, it belches with acid of putting food into the mouth steadily over the years, synthetic fabrication of cranked up minutes, droning scales of hours chewing on the vital functions, which are now the size of mashed up peas.

118

Nevertheless she ignores this dust gathered so, throws it like a dishcloth into the dustbin from where it will crawl out in the morning. I follow her, trying hard not to trip over the small abandoned porcelain tidbits on the floor. I know this is never going to repeat. She invites me for a cup of tea, and then we enter her paintings. There are the grey empty wombs of death, with her twisted hungering fingers of pain. We dive into its terrors, its layers of breakdown. There are also her dreams, the soothing paws of tigers. I have their amber eyes in my sockets. We emerge from the asylum for the girls unadjusted, unadjusted still, but in one piece. We are two small points bobbing up and down on the cold summer sea under the colossal chair with a giant skeleton of Buddha, his decomposing skin loosely hanging on the skull, blown out of his bones, bones corroded, he sits there, laughing and laughing into the eternity, that withered jaw, spelling out the joke of existence. The ice of words reaches further, we find it right on the stairs that lead out, somewhere. Out. But step there, regardless.

Petra Whiteley

Do The Black Poppies Still Hear You Sing
for Sylvia Plath

Sylvia Plath
you   were   the first
poet
I fell in love with.

I followed you down
through long-- twisting-- tunnels.
I walked barefoot
across shards of black-broken glass
----mixed my blood with your blood---

I tore words from your books.
Ate them.   My appetite was ferocious.

You were the thread
that stitched me into my dark side.
You were the raw wind
that swirled to devour and suffocate   (me.)
Even as I struggled-----not to be consumed------
you taught me how-to-dance into
my own Voice.

I could end this poem right here
but I still hold your song in my throat
and in my right hand I clutch a cluster of black poppies
and in my left hand   shadows fill a jagged-mirror
that cuts deeply into my flesh.

So I stand here in the soft-mud of our pain-mixed-blood
and within my own (strong)   heartbeat
I stretch out to embrace   and lift my tongue skyward
to catch the wonderment of you   slowly dripping
drop   by drop   by drop   into my mouth.

Peggy Anne Larson

120

Musemagik*

According to my writer-friend Magda
her muse
wears an ethereal, cascading veil
sparkle of star
silken plume of quail
This muse speaks in sparrow
and murmurs
in dialect of dove
cautioning her
that His rainbows are but mirage
"See" she whispers
(not in language of man)
"how they melt
in Mother Nature's mouth of rain..."
A Lady of silent intensity:
A telepathic banshee
(of unseen beauty)
who flails her arms and voice
in a bloodjet of ideas...
The fingers of her muse
death's head
moths
fluttering under her skin,
Magda's soul again and again
awakens to the abrupt arrival,
feeling like--
a cobra
facing a mongoose
whose fur stands on end as it lunges--
the only truth
bleeds from that moment
into...
her...
pen...

Gloria J. Wimberley

121

Confessions: III

It isn't late
only about eight
I'm in bed
avoiding,

              propped in position
by a credulous number of pillows
and over-stuffed cushions.
I am not full of feathers
or food
or wine.

The baby is sleeping next door,
every now and then shifting
and I become still
a breath lingering on my lips,
then she settles.
I exhale and cast my eyes back down
towards words
        spilling over words.

I am surround by sustenance;
notebooks,
crumpled newspapers of the day
books - half written poems,
confessions scribbled on scraps
of paper.
I shall curse myself later
when I realise I threw them out,
or that they have been sucked to death
as I pick the pulp out of her mouth.

Her need to taste the world is foreign to me.

I am waiting for the evacuation
of myself
from myself.
Later...

The clock flashes
through an orange glowing dark,
street lamps bruise the curtains,
I can't make out the time.
My eyes sting
ears straining in case the baby is stirring,
needs milk
            or comfort
                        or me.

I can hear my insides ripple
a crippling grasp of cramp
runs from sternum to pubic bone
and back again.
            Ah, here it comes,
a sense of relief
washes over me,
tiredness pulls at my bones
weighting me,
gravity refusing to give up her possession.

One day I may be weightless
like the woman
who always dreamed she was flying,
I was always jealous.

Here it comes again
            my demon and her vengeance,
my body   turning   on my body
as if it has done itself a terrible wrong.

I regret for a moment
my earlier choices,
before the pain comes
and its reward seems too far away,
a vision on the periphery
of my reality.
Sunrise is hours away
and I never did like the dark.

It's early
too early and I am spent,
exhaustion has crept into the spaces
I have made,
claws at the empty pit of my stomach
irritated and irrational.
We are strange bed fellow
but cannot stop sharing my bed
in our bare nakedness.

She is stirring,
cooing to herself
she'll be wanting breakfast soon,
my daughter sounds happy   contented,
practicing her voice.
I listen and smile at her fullness,
close my eyes for a moment
to feign sleep
         to   drift   away,
before setting my feet on the blue carpet,
before walking to her
to say good morning,
         before putting my demons away.

Samantha Ledger

Woven Into Me

We were the possibility of womanhood,
 the possibility of witches,
gathered like threads of string
woven into patterns.

I remember us, our fingers on the cup
that slid across the Ouija board.
Annie said I'd moved it, no one disagreed.

We grew like reeds among the sand dunes,
by the bay and near the rivers.
We moved in a pack. We held together.

With my sister I climbed hay bales in the old barn,
covered in dust and shadows. At night
she woke me for adventures,
picking our way down to a river between fir trees.
She told me ghost stories beginning

     'This Is All True'

and I believed her.
It's so long ago and I am buried well inside
my grown-up body.

I can fill myself up with memories
of fresh faces pale in northern winters,
long hair and skinny elbows, all
of us in that landscape, in that light.

But mostly I let it all sit silently behind my ribcage
to be discovered when I am old
and need to dream.

Sophia Argyris

Clairvoyant

She is the Death card
held tightly between
index and thumb

dry flowers growing soft
in stagnant water, heads bowed
like funeral shadows upon vibrant green

she is runes and ancient stones,
heavy darkness laid like cloth
upon wooden slats in the dim

spells spoken, eyes tightly fastened
glowing wax burning in meditation,
elements fused to spirals and alchemy

she is gypsy magic and moonglow,
black prayer and pentagons,
nine lives counted in skulls, four corners

smoke of burning sage,
shell of abalone raised to deaf gods
chanting breath of new blood

she is anointed oil on palms
scarlet linen stretched tight,
petrified rosewood, obsidian

hooves of sacred beasts,
ornate mirrors, morphing reflections,
red wine spilling forth

she is kindling and wet ash
soot clinging to walls like new demons,
paper angels folded in reverence

a Cyclops of clarity and vision
movement of shadows in the still
wandering souls of familiars

 she is black cats and superstition,
spider and hourglass,
harvest moon, the number 13

swallowing silence, belief,
cauldrons and cawing crows, equinox
and solstice imprisoned in a jar

she is sickles and sewn eyelids
shutters clamoring through silence
blackwater and sacrifice on the bayou

spent matches and sulfur flame,
a sepulcher of bent knees and clasped hands,
veiled mistress of midnight

she is circle, oracle, orb,
painted faces, symbolic sculptures,
congregation of wolf and owl

howling wind and window panes,
bloodstains on a Persian rug,
lifelines interpreted, repeated, prophetic.

She is clairvoyant.

Apryl Skies

On The Conjuring Of Devils

She is angry and indiscreet—a minor poet
who gets emails from happy Christian folk damning her

for daring to suggest that there are a million paths
to the Light, that a white bird may be other than a

symbol of the Holy Spirit, that crucifixion
is a daily occurrence, that Jesus may not like

any of us very much. Something is taking place
around her, that much is certain. She struggles with Oil

of Olay's delusion of beauty and imagines
the irregular heartbeat, the longing for peace, and

an end to the language of superfluous destruction.
Hear those songs? purring, articulating, crackling,

gurgling, dry as old orchards, rain-swept as seas, and nearly
always claiming the lie of incomprehension.

Her children smile — their beautiful condescension
falls on her, soaking her. They think she conjures devils

where there are none. Her friends choke on her love
for William Clinton — her respect for his ability

to appreciate a good blow job nearly as much
as a well-written treaty. Her husband admires her
blatancy. She decided long ago that there would
be no "last songs," only tunes of passage. No doubt

about it, her behavior is outrageous, ribald,
pornographic. She uses the "f" word out loud.

Her daughter asked her — years earlier (voice dripping with
teenage sarcasm) — as menopause descended,

"Mother, are you going to take long walks now out in the fields and think deep
thoughts among the wildflowers?"

They both laughed, but the writer of songs blushed
lavender red. Thinking deep thoughts among the wildflowers
as she walked through fields had been her practice all her life.

She dislikes late afternoons and headaches, cringes at
unkindness, eats too much. The songs catch her at all the

inconvenient moments: in the supermarket, the
elevator, the gym — in the middle of sit-ups

for gods sakes. Her hazardous incentives make her
wakeful, the cold damp weather she loves makes her knees hurt,

the mirrors she cleans with newspaper and vinegar
reflect all she does not wish to see. Still, she writes songs

of Stonehenge and South L.A., black coffee and bleak seasons.
In her sleep, wind chimes sing her songs back to her. They are loud.

Quickly, quickly while it's light
Stillness threatens evening's fright.

Martina Reisz Newberry

Vanda

Bleeding cries of death's lullabies
shatter the morning calm
there is no escaping death
or the soft turn of dawn's light
spun to feeble hands and breathless

    --still--

among a manic stumble of pleas
dreams turn dark, reality darker
and black suits are coming
red ants marching onward
for this silent vessel, that
no longer reads the palms
seeking answers from the universe
no longer is this (real)m home

Her corpse lies cold
beneath fleece blankets
stale and still, hands stiff like stones
eyes fixed upon the gates of heaven
or nowhere at all, I can't be certain,
my faith in these things
is marked by question
broken like pottery, held like sacrament
against a somber refrain
and the ravens have come
dressed like black Sunday

She is a signature on a framed certificate,
ether or ash, an amethyst sky
burned into the psyche

She is a fucking memory…

Apryl Skies

Beneath Silence

Guilt rises, ebbing
like bile from my stomach
I crawl forth through an endless winter
embracing jagged Frost
It claws with vengeance up my spine
whispers in my ear

Spring has died and Autumn lost
your precious Summer ever-stained
for this your muted sin's to blame
and in the Dead of Night she crossed...

Survival is a stagnant creek pooling at my clavicle
teeming with all the putrid life I still have yet to live
standing here in this steel gray winter
holding out my pound of flesh
to the ancient specter of a dream
I want the world to know.
To hear my strangled scream.
But fog surrounds
it fills my lungs and laces breath with pain
breathing in and bleeding out
beneath my silence lies the shame...

Silver Corbin

brokenwing
for edie

"we all have wings to soar & fly beneath a vast poetic sky..."

you were floating face up when you were found--
locked, rigid, embalmed in frigid waters breaking
quietly upon the shallow shores of the Chesapeake Bay

small sparrow broken, thin arms askew, identifiable
only by a downy halo brushing softly against a pale
countenance so serene, one might imagine you dreaming,
but your dreams died long ago... When

faith was shattered by those you once thought mattered

left lonely in a nest emptied of fledglings flown--
a song bird silenced, lustrous plumage dulled with time,
coolly abandoned by an inattentive handler of transient affection

for flesh, like feathers will fall with the passing of seasons

and you, small creature, passed many a season behind skillfully
applied smiles, peacock feather eyes designed to disguise anxieties
roiling beneath a quivering breast, lying now, naked, cold as winter,
grounded by gnashing vultures striping from you your youth,
your truth, chewing, feeding both to their young, your

vulnerabilities bared by those you once thought cared

convinced in your despair that they did not...

what tipped the precarious balance you struggled to maintain,
the sanity you desperately fought to retain resolutely forfeited,
reluctantly released into placid Maryland waters...how, little bird—

did I so miserably fail to see that reflection in your eyes
of an infinite sky where all wild things, even those with broken wings,
soar high, unshackled from sorrow and *free?*

Alicia Winski

134

Cat Eyes and the Tragedy of Mother

Could I marry these two sharp silences? These yellow balls
that burn in stare and purr beneath
deep where the world is simple.

Are they cat eyes or a brace of grief's fresh
from the hunter's recreation?

Will they say, *I do*? Two ochre brides
with their black faces and their undercurrent of woe. Cat

eyes are everything
like newborn infants that have barely tasted the world.

How can we know without tragedy? All the broken
birds and mouse heads merely death's decoration
like my mother's trousseau and her years of mending only

to be lost in the stitches
and the thread falling away
her bloody thumb a jewel. She married a ductile grief

its lifeline on her palm
the law of its docile acquiescence
that lifted only to plug the hollow of my despair. The day she died

my wasted roots fell away
and I was born again like an inconsolable thunder.

Gillian Prew

Regressions: IV

About the room lay the remains of another day
abandonment looms underneath shadows,
toys discarded and nimble hands
sleep now- as fists ,
a mouth sucking them furiously.

My child often displays cannibalistic tendencies
yet the delicacies she shows
are foreign to me,
her father cannot comment
having drifted out to sea
on the wreckage of a marriage,
never made but marred
over two borders long divided.

Dis-ord-er-ed

I am (our) burnt carcass
turning in dim light
of a diminishing day,
my shadow thin-
under nourished
a ring finger bare to the bone.

There is a shift in time
            splitting
                    spitting
I lay
head buried under
a scent of remembrance,
the sickle moon
moves across my abdomen
tracing lines from where she came
and he left an indelible mark.

What am I if not a woman-
a belittling cry of motherhood
rests trapped in a ring box
high on a dusty shelf,
always out of reach.
My fingers are stubs
wrists arthritic,
my skin has turned
to hues of grey-blue.
This heart resent the effort
it
          must
                    undertake
in beating.

The bleeding cornice of thorns-
stinging nettles and willow- sits beautifully
atop a head that hangs limply to the side,
the tide drags out another breath
as I am pulled under -
into a savage unconscious slumber.

Samantha Ledger

The Great Escape

Goddamn you~

Slipping out the easy way, leaving behind nothing more than
recrimination, condemnation, vile, vicious accusation of
the family you divided with your Nazi-like ideology,
separating the pure from the impure, your own personal
war crimes against your blood *and yet*

I can't walk past your door without wanting to call in,
"Hi, mother, how are you doing?"

knowing damn well I'd hear nothing more than complaints
of pain and dark ponderings of death lightened only by
the occasional chirp of laughter making the whole dismal
conversation worth that one precious moment of calm,
when I could call you "Mom" without qualm or reservation

Where did you go to,
that woman I thought I knew?

Are you finally in hell or lying in limbo
waiting for redemption you'll never receive?

Perhaps you're simply a noxious vapor in the air, slowly
poisoning the innocent and pure of heart as you did of those
you spawned *and yet ...*

> *why is it I miss you?*

Is it because you were the only constant in the world of
a lost little girl used and abused by those you gave your
silent permission to?

Could it be because of the, oh, so occasional, walk about town,
when you held a tiny hand, tolerating girlish chatter in rhythm
with the high heels clicking down a flawed, cracked sidewalk?

> *Such an appropriate path for you and I!*

I walk alone now through a house grown emptier by the moment,
fingers trailing over dusty remnants of your life, contemplating
all the lies spoon fed to me from birth, stopping at the foot of
your cold bed, a bed you were deprived of at death, whispering

"I miss you so much"
      to a mama that never existed

Alicia Winski

Mommy

Mommy was the face on the barroom floor
in a poem by George Robert Sims
we didn't touch , mommy and me
I didn't know how
and she didn't want to
but we wore the same face in our lives

Once she brought me a see-through nightgown
to the maternity ward
I can't wear this I thought

"I have to conform, she said,
walk barefoot on the grass for me."

Lois Michal Unger

Hands

Our hands and their hold
the first touch upon new skin
can heal or destroy

Apryl Skies

Dear Mother

We were close once
before the harsh divide
before the ceaseless
sparring of our wills

I've been told
the first few years
can make or
break a child

I plucked
the morning glory
from your vine
and I remember

Barbara Moore

Forgiveness on the Tongue

"What...near my voice"
Zillah thought she heard softly
in a softer head-cloud
of a dream...

Her Kyoko, sultry,
even after their thorntwist aria
of a fight
spoke
focused
and breathy
as a bamboo reed,
which trembles
ever so slightly in
morning's
mouth
of
jade-green mist
and honeyed dew

...how crisp & clean the taste
of mercy

Gloria J. Wimberley

In Aftermath

I found a picture of you today

a singular treasure hidden within the deep, dark recesses
of a cheap camera I forgot I owned; a little red Kodak
long buried in a drawer filled with a lifetime of memorabilia--

> *letters of passion, crayoned portraits, tiny*
> *tooth fairy teeth and locks of my loves*

I nearly dropped it, finding myself rooted in spot staring into
pretty hazel eyes; your eyes, those painfully confused eyes
once holding a thousand promises, now

> *holding nothing more than*
> *a thousand goodbyes*

your queenly beautiful warrior's face, still maintaining remarkable
grace in a stand-off with a cruel, lethal adversity; you, a feminine
David, to an unseen Goliath gone to battle; slowly, surely, losing

> *a war all familial soldiers knew--*
> *would never be won*

with my fingers, I traced over your smile, a smile once holding the
power to break a man's heart; now pursed, thinly disguised under
that atrocious salmon color I teased you about, laughing unmercifully

as I told you it was a shade suited only to hookers or the blue-haired
geriatric regime seeking asylum, and taking refuge in the sanctuary
of your small town, but

> *your hair was silver, wasn't it? I had forgotten--*
> *how could I have forgotten?*

that hair; your one real vanity, gone limp with disease; I cried when
I remembered the lifeless dulled strands left behind in my comb as
I slid it through, all the while assuring you of its remaining beauty, but

> *I lied; its beauty had long since*
> *faded ... away*

overwhelmed by the intricacies of your dance with death,
I condemned myself for squandering lost, precious time with you,
time spent, instead, with solitude, knowing in that moment

I would have given up a year of my solitary life if only--
> *to hand you back one of your own*

I found a picture of you today, but upon somber reflection,
put it away, back to the drawer housing

> *the rest*
> *of my regrets*

Alicia Winski

In All Fairness

To my mother & our "cushy" life. Thank you. My love for you is a deep well…

My mother always said, "Life isn't fair." This was my mother's method of teaching me to tough things out and she would certainly know better than anyone about life's many grievances.

She lost a husband, a sister, a brother, two children and both her parents. She raised children that weren't hers and never faltered, never once carried resentment, never once revealed fear… I have yet to see my mother shed a tear.

My mother taught me to carry a sense of dignity in one pocket and humility in the other. She taught me compassion and generosity, even when what I have to offer isn't a lot. My mother strongly believed in hand-me-downs, carpools and Sunday school, these were the ingredients for childhood, resiliency and survival.

In all fairness, my mother was right about most things and she was certainly correct with her words of wisdom…

"Sometimes, life just isn't fair."

Mother swept
the floor of our sorrow
always without shame.

The breached womb,
a breathless child
the porcelain basin where
the downward daughter
lies lifeless;
our stark truths tainting cold
the bathroom tile.

The crimson stain
of innocence lost,
the stolen locket of purity
ripped away

Rosary beads, red and sacred
scatter to the creaking floorboards
and reveal our secrets, our pain
and our laughter too.

Mother swept
the floor of our pain
always without shame
and somehow always
sees the sunshine through the rain.

Apryl Skies

Coming Home

The car sailed,
in the rushing hour
of sixteen lanes,
whispered thoughts –

"I'm going to die"

I said thanks to God.
I had just left the children
this clear, sunny day.
Before clear turned to black
and light and black again.
No steering or fighting,
but screeches and rubber burning;
steel on steel,
steel on flesh.
Here and gone;
gone again.

Pulled within an aura,
the grace of She
I missed so long.
Sun in my hair
I dropped the rod
and skipped the tall grass
like a child called home.

Grandma, I think- holding my hand.
No breath, no sound
cloaked in white haze,
skipping on hurried feet.
Gay meadow.

But, what voices?
Distant..... "Mommy"

Calling..... "Mommy"...
and She - smiled.

Tugged,
from light toward dark again,
and sudden breath.

Muffled voices, shuffles, cries
heard within but distant still
my whisper for days...

"I won't leave you"
"I won't leave you"

From dark to light
and in their aura.
Aura all around...
I'm coming home.

Catharine Grasty

Getting to the Heart of the Matter

Beauty moves me within
shifts my senses
makes me stop and think
Beauty is finding something
strong and special
in the weak and artificial

To show others what I see
through my eyes
to show them what is beautiful
within the dark and ugly

show them who I am
search for a deeper meaning
trite as that sounds
to strip the surface emotions
and get down to the heart of the matter

I don't know.
I just know that I have to go on.
there's something more out there
that goes beyond the reach of hardship
there is something
just within my grasp
and I have to keep reaching for it
or die spiritually and emotionally

I'm not willing to die yet

Alicia Winski

In The Company of Women

When I was younger, I had very little regard for women, probably because of my mother's aversion to them. She and her mother had not been close, and I believe she spent the first third of her life in search of an elusive female confidante. She thought that, with proper indoctrination, I could grow into that role. I was taught that men were worthy candidates for friendship, whereas women were never to be trusted. My early sense of reality was shaped by my mother's views. It wasn't until a severing of our mother-daughter relationship that I began to detach from her teachings and embrace my own reality-based truths. My appreciation for men remains, but the understanding, support and sheer joy I experience within the realm of sisterhood grows with each new shared experience.

In gray flowered gowns
that open in the front
we sit flipping pages
in outdated magazines

We are body language
and competing heart beats
weary warriors
with amputated words

Our thought plugs have been pulled
our minds drained/emptied
where statistics once marched
in battle fatigues

The elephant in the room
is armed with breastplates
Each time a woman's name is called
we hurl our collective breath

Barbara Moore

My Breast

You nurtured
gave pleasure.

Changed,
harbored
a secret weapon.

Disarmed in time,
I look at you now,
telltale scar
frowns.

I pat you down,
not gently,
lump rising only
in my throat,
this time.

Cristina Umpfenbach-Smyth

Mimic

Under this moon I feel you,
penetrating my smile,
cleansing my cheek with a gentle finger
reflecting your spirit on my body.
It deepens –
saturating me with love.

When I'm out here
in the jungle
you tell me not to weep
because a tear
could water the
things around me,
absorbing me,
like a weed
near a flower.

I look up for you –
in a deep faint sky.
No stars but the moon,
a gentle whistle of brightness
above me.
Where are you
in the heavens beyond my eyes–
these brown,
swollen eyes?

You were the first to go.
The first to engrave
our name in the stars.
The last-born
and first enthroned,
kneeling below the innocent

Virgin,
whispering secrets
amongst the wisest known.

You were made a martyr
to a force you knew well.
Forceful, slow,
weakening.
Absorbing your yawns,
your sighs,
your sneezes,
until the last muffle
was quieted.

I stay here beneath you,
sheltered by your umbrella.
Dancing over cancer puddles,
angry at what you died for.

I want it to mimic
the shaking of your limbs,
the way your cheeks
became peaks,
and your mouth
an oasis
to no
more
words.

Where can I find you
where I stand,
to greet you in embrace
and ask you for the answers
to your disease?
In each wrinkle of my shirt

I can see your crinkled nose
laughing
at my puzzlement.
Wondering
why I haven't figured
out your riddle by now.

"Why do you search
for me above you,
when I'm right
inside you?
Sharing the same face
and the same name."

Jessica Wilson

Saying Goodbye

How stoic and smiling you were,
murmuring gentle encouragement
as the clumsy fingered Nurse
filled your port with poison.

Your thin shiny lips, once so full;
curled with relief and pleasure as
the sedative rode in on the current.
Sickening sweet scent of insecticide filled the air.

Later, riding home in the car,
you opened the window.
The rain splashed your face and you laughed,
saying you thought it went well today.

Once they had finished ravaging you,
after you surrendered.
We said goodbye for days.
You held court and visitors wept in fine fashion.

You made all your plans,
checked off your many lists and
went to bed with your final lover.
Your morphine friend stilled you.

Five weeks later, after no food or water had
passed your lips, leaving your tongue like
a twisted piece of dried leather.
No longer waking only moaning,

I stopped saying goodbye
and begged for God
                    ...for anyone
to hurry up and finish the fucking job.

Lauri Langston

156

'night Mother

The soft hum and hiss
of machines in the night
mingling with labored breaths
and medicinal fumes
wafting beneath my nose

Appalled by the cruelty
of life slowly dissipating
before me,

Echoes of goodbyes
fill the empty halls
[closing in on me]
Skin, once bright,
now gray with disease
Red-rimmed eyes dim
in the glow of blinking lights
where girlish dreams,
once vibrant, fade away
along with her life.

Knowing her end is near,
riddled with fear,
my sorrows trickle
onto her beloved face…

Death's hands hold no grace

I lean down to kiss
dry, cracked lips
My broken whispers
pressed against a deaf ear

'night Mother…

Alicia Winski

157

For Alicia

When our hearts
cannot find words
and the path to peace
descends long and deep,
may we find our voice
among the hillside's distant blooms

When our eyes run dry of tears
and we are lost
in a haze of uncertainty
may the clouds weep for us
washing us relieved

And when our souls are heavy
with the burden of our grieving,
may hope lift us to our weary feet

When we find ourselves alone
in the weakness of our frailty
may we find a friend full of light
to shed the rendering of our pain

When our brothers mourn
and our sister's faces
are drowned in tears,
may I be that shining sun
upon the hillside's tender petals
in their beautiful, grinning,
gold relief...

And call myself a friend.

The Mathematics of Division

I grew up in a vanilla-flavored ice cream cone
of family secrets,
to be slowly licked away,
tears shamed away to dark hidden places
while my grandmother held Jesus deep in her heart
and stoned people with her words
eating my soul with glinting eyes,
blood dripping onto her Sunday-Best-Dress.

In this invisible emptiness
tiny zeros slice through nothing.
No alphabet here, no markings
to form language,   only
the ovalness of flesh forgotten
and droplets of sound   waiting
patiently
waiting.

Hidden in this slice of time
her lipstick smeared graffiti
still stands guard,
slow shadows still sway
across folded papers stitched tight
with the dust of deep secrets.
Here among this clutter of mix-messages
a music box sits stranded   silent   waiting

waiting for tender hands
to lift its heart into the light,
into a small basket of fragrant soft-petaled-colors.
and   maybe   even   into an illusion
of its own fragile-scented beauty.

Peggy Anne Larson

In the Company of Women

The time has come for my thoughts on In The Company of Women, ones I've found impossible to lasso or capture onto paper... until the moment I sat, red pen in hand, with a collection of work so dazzling and touching, I knew nothing I said would speak louder or more thoroughly than the words I held in my hand.

I have sisters the world over and they have spoken for me. Pam Lampe touched me with her submission, a shy comment to us at Edgar and Lenore's, "I'm not a poet, but I thought I had something to say". She was wrong. She is a poet and has much to say. Annie Brodrick, who quietly waited in wings wondering if we would find her work publishable. We did. Lois Michal Unger questioned if she had any work that would fit well into the theme of this anthology and is one of the strongest threads tying this beautiful word-quilt together. Also, Cklara Moradian who raised her fist and voice singing a song of freedom and survival. Cristina Umpfenbach-Smyth, a hero, who tells of her battle with cancer in words of such grace and humor, I am in awe. Sheila Crawford whose love letter to her little ones is a thread holding the concept of feminine unity together. Pd Lietz, who so struggled to find her voice in this crowd of beauties and when she did, moved me with a simple ode to a friend. Most importantly, I have my friend and soul sister, Apryl Skies, a compact, fiery little tiger who, with depth and insight far beyond her years and a heart full of dreams, fought like hell to keep me grounded when I would let life sweep me away, all the while teaching me that friendship has no price.

This incredible collective of strong women, friends and sisters, *so* many not named here, have lead me, often kicking and screaming, down a road paved in tears, laughter, heartache and many a loving bump, to a place of faith and trust I never thought I'd find. Surviving adversity even the strongest of men have fallen beneath; neglect, poverty, war, abuse, incest, violence and disease, all with integrity, compassion, humor and belief intact. In doing so, have welcomed me into their company, despite an upbringing housed in distrust and fear; despite lonely, dream-some days, hiding behind music, books and writing, have shown me that when I'm caged in self doubt, and floundering in uncertainty, when life is at its darkest, the brightest of lights and laughter can always be found, In The Company of Women and really, what more can one say?   *...Ladies, I salute you!*

In a life often filled with sadness and pain,
I've found so little to trust, much less to gain
in the company of women...

I've found little compassion, in what now seems the fashion
of sisters commiserating, feeding off each other's miseries...

> *So many I've met were vicious vipers,*
> *snipers, bitchy and verbal fighters*
> *ready to take me on, shoot me down,*
> ***--snap sharply--*** *at my Achilles heel*

dark, frightening mysteries I never could comprehend,
muting me by distrust, a silent wary observer, although...
when crucified by contempt, view clouded to hopeful horizons,
lost and disconnected by despair, finding me low...

> *my interest was caught by conversation fraught*
> *with good humor and gentle chiding...*

it was in the arms and hearts of women
I now call *friend*, lifting me high,
sisters, friends, have proven by and by...

> *herculean ears may lie deaf to fears, when broken*
> *hearts shunned by the virile, a woman, once held*
> *captive behind locked jaw and blinded eye*
> *may salvage dream swept ships run aground, resettled*
> *and moored in safe harbors found, often only —*

In The Company of Women

> *~start paddling ladies...*

Alicia Winski

161

Acknowledgements

Unless otherwise stated all, photographs are courtesy of the U.S. Library of Congress - Public domain, all rights reserved.

Breath Beneath the Surface - Photo courtesy of Wanda Morrow Clevenger

My Unsung Heroine - Photo courtesy of Cklara Moradian

A Blood Bloom to Hold – Photo of Seattle Tulip by Apryl Skies

My Love - photo courtesy of Sheila Crawford

Dear Mother – Photo of Nature's Juxtapose by Apryl Skies

In All Fairness – Photo Mother courtesy of Apryl Skies

brokenwing - In Memory of Edie, who had the ability and insight to recognize even the most hidden pain in others. If only I had the same gifts…When Edie's body was found and her car recovered, her family found, among her personal effects, a signed copy of my book *Running on Fumes,* which I had given to her as a gift. The night after I gave it to her, she came to me, held my hand and quietly stated, "You've been hurt haven't you?"   …*Fly among angels my friend~*

brokenwing - beginning quote by Apryl Skies

www.EdgarAllanPoet.com

www.ingramcontent.com/pod-product-compliance
Lightning Source LLC
Chambersburg PA
CBHW080734250626
47170CB00010B/2828